HOW TO FULFIL
DIVINE PURPOSE

HOW TO FULFIL DIVINE PURPOSE

The Quest of All Mankind

MKO OYENEYE

Rev. date: 06/24/2019

To order additional copies of this book, contact:
Xlibris
1-888-795-4274
www.Xlibris.com
Orders@Xlibris.com
798738

CONTENTS

"You could reach all your personal goals, becoming a raving success by the world's standard, and still miss the purpose for which God created you...
You were created by God and for God – and until you understand that, life will never make sense".
Rick Warren

DEDICATION

To the human heart for renewal and transformation.

To every individual given birth by destiny for divine assignment and fulfilment of purpose.

To the one who finds life empty, aimless and busy but not effective.

To you, the reader. For whom I desire a purposeful life characterised by effectiveness, efficiency, fulfilment and eternal rewards.

To all who are oppressed by the ignorance of others.

To every generation that seeks meaning and reasons for living.

To everyone who is seeking for himself/herself.

ACKNOWLEDGMENTS

WE ARE THE sum total of what we have learned from all who have taught us, both great and small. I am grateful for the inspirations and wisdom of great men and women of God and Authors for the transgenerational sources and roots of wisdom and knowledge they have transferred to me.

I am also grateful for all men and brethren, members, friends and colleagues at Jubilee Christian Church International – JCCI Worldwide (Particularly: Jubilee International Bible Institute where I began this teaching) whose faithfulness and prayers continuously influence me to continue to fulfil my purpose and potentials in life.

For the development and production of this book itself, I feel a deep sense of gratitude to:

> My precious wife and life-time best-friend, Bernice Aderayo Omotoke (Nee Soetan) who I fondly called 'Ayamitoke' and our children and grandchild, Samuel, Dorcas and Emmanuel; our daughter and son-in-law, Joy and Kenny for supports all through the journey of life thus far. You make it easier to fulfil God's will for my life.

My late father and mother, Chief
Solomon and Madam Janet

Abebi Oyeneye; for their devotion to the Lord and to their children, and for their constant demonstration of love that inspired me to pursue the discovery and fulfilment of my purpose.

My siblings: Mrs Felicia Abimbola, Mrs Elizabeth Koya, Aare Tunde Oyeneye and Mrs Awero Mulero.

My dear friend and destiny helpers, Dr Gordon Hurd and his beloved wife - whose commitment to the work and vision makes this project possible.

Dr Sunday Adelaja of the Embassy of The Blessed Kingdom of God Church for all Nations in Ukraine for his Transformational Teachings as well as History Makers Training – HMT and Mentorship Programmes.

Last but not the least: Rev Dr Kunle & Rev Mrs Felicia Adesina, General Overseer of JCCI Worldwide by Grace for giving all of us the platform to serve the Lord Our Jubilee thereby finding our fulfilment in HIM.

FOREWORD

WHEN PASTOR MKO asked me to preface his latest book *How To Fulfil Divine Purpose*, I was excited that yet another servant of God has caught the vision to inspire God's children to seriously consider the reason they were created in the first place.

Throughout all my years in ministry, my saddest moments have arisen when I ponder the sheer waste of God-given talent in the Kingdom. I have seen great men and women endowed with so much wisdom, intellect, energy and talent, waste away their lives in trivial pursuits.

Thankfully, I have also watched young Christians come into the church, caught a divine purpose and gone on to impact the world in a positive way. Pastor MKO is a shining example!

For those of you who may be struggling with locating or fulfilling your vision, there is hope. This book is not in your hand by chance. It is a clarion call to from the Maker of the universe to arise and take your position in this world.

One thing I love about *How To Fulfil Divine Purpose* is the fact that it is written with clarity and simplicity and provides a simple, yet effective, road map to finding and fulfilling your divine purpose. Read it many times until it becomes clear to you what you are assigned to do in this world and how you should do it.

My own life in Ministry reminds me every day that I would have been miserable if I had not heeded the call to service of our Master Jesus Christ. However, your calling need not mimic mine nor the author's. You are unique and your divine purpose may be in another field that is completely different from the obvious calling of a servant of God. Whatever it is, carry out your purpose as unto God and not unto man.

I would like to thank Pastor MKO for writing this book and making available another great life manual to the Kingdom. I pray that after *How To Fulfil Divine Purpose*, he will be led to write many other inspiring books that will shape the life of Christians and non-Christians alike in generations to come.

May you be truly blessed as you read this book.

Rev. Dr. Adekunle Adesina
General Overseer JCCI worldwide

INTRODUCTION

ONE OF THE things that have bothered me since I started in ministry is the fact that Man does not use his God-given potential. The more I study and pray, the more it becomes clear that the missing ingredient is the absence of a roadmap that would take us to our purpose.

A car functions well as a car, not as a heater. A microwave functions well as a microwave, not as a fridge. Sadly, a lot of people, including God's children, function out of the original plan of the Master and so fail to express their full potential.

This book seeks to address that imbalance.

Living life without a purpose is not only ill-advised; it is dangerous. Here is what Dr. Jim White has to say about living life without a compass:

> "A life without a purpose is a life without a destination. Like a boat adrift on the ocean, there is no telling where you might end up. With no direction to your life, you will be moved by random feelings and emotions into any harbour. Two thousand years ago the Roman philosopher Seneca wrote, "Our plans miscarry because they have no aim. When a man does not know what harbour he is making for, no wind is the right wind." Adrift at the mercy of random feelings or unidentified urges, you will be capable of any evil because you lack control of your own life. Purpose provides a vision that leads you to a vocation rather than to a mere job. It provides for passion and meaning to replace tedium and aimlessness. The question 'Why Am I Here?' goes much deeper than finding what career is best for you. Finding a

purpose is ultimately a spiritual endeavour because it involves
a process of connecting with something greater than yourself".

I totally agree.

In the following pages we will go on a quest with you to try to locate the reason why you came to earth in the first place.

In Chapter 1, we explore the definition and characteristics of purpose and raise some controversial issues surrounding the subject.

In Chapter 2, we look at Man as God's original purpose and the implications of being created by a God that rules the entire universe.

In Chapter 3, we study some of the hindrances to discovering your purpose and propose a way out.

In Chapter 4, we look at God's plan of redemption through Christ and posit that even though Man may have fallen, there is hope of a new life of purpose through the resurrection of Jesus Christ.

In Chapter 5, we zero in on how people find their purpose in life, walked in their purpose and changed the course of history. We discuss purpose by divine appointment and deliberate creation.

In Chapters 6, 7 and 8, we bring in some vital and key ingredients including principles to manifesting your purpose as you navigate through the choppy waters of life.

In Chapter 9, we state that your purpose is your divine assignment as present men and women past and present who have walked in their purpose and changed the course of history.

In Chapter 10, we highlight the role of purpose helpers and purpose killers and show how the former can help catapult you into your life purpose while the latter can sink your ship before it even leaves the harbour.

In Chapter 11, we enjoin you to wait on the Lord and be thankful for your current situation, knowing that the vision is for the appointed time and in the end, it shall speak.

In Chapter 12, we throw down the gauntlet of divine purpose before you and dare you to wake up and live according to your God-given plan.

How to Fulfil Divine Purpose is not just a book. It is a dare. As you read it, I dare you to look in the mirror and ask yourself why you are really here. The Lord Himself will speak to you. When He does, be ready to take bold, uncompromising action. Remember, it is never too late to move in the right direction simply because you think you have gone too far. William Danforth tells the story of a bus conductor in Canada who worked on the streets for 20 years before it dawned on him that he was created for far greater things. He changed direction and became a General in the army.

May your divine purpose be made manifest as you read this book.

MKO Oyeneye
Senior Pastor: JCCI Faith Arena, UK
Regional Coordinator JCCI UK/EUROPE
Assistant General Overseer (Finance) JCCI

PART I

UNDERSTANDING
DIVINE PURPOSE

CHAPTER 1

THE DEFINITION AND CHARACTERISTICS OF PURPOSE

**"You were put on this earth to achieve your
greatest self, to live out your purpose,
and to do it courageously." Steve Maraboli**

IN THIS CHAPTER, we will explore the true meaning of purpose. We will also take a cursory look at the extraordinary qualities with which Man is endowed. Finally, we will wade into the controversy surrounding purpose.

What is the Meaning of Purpose?

Purpose can be defined as the reason for which something is done or created. Or the reason why something exists. The French would call it the "raison d'être". Synonyms of purpose include motive, motivation, grounds, cause, impetus, reason, point, basis, target, ambition, objective and justification.

Purpose is derived from the Old French *porpos*, from the verb *porposer*, (to put forth) a variant of **proposer**. Put very simply, a purpose is what somebody wants to do or become. It is the end goal or endpoint of somebody's toil and travail. When someone enters university, their goal is one of the many options available at his institution of choice. The person's purpose at the end of their sojourn at the university is to prove that they went through university by achieving a BA, MA or PhD.

When a climber heads for Mount Everest, their purpose is to reach the summit and add their name to the record of those that have performed that perilous, yet heroic feat.

The purpose of a pregnancy is to bring forth a baby after 9 months. There is no joy in an everlasting pregnancy and you can verify this by asking any woman who has gone one day beyond their due date.

An athlete's goal or purpose is to reach the finishing line and win the trophy. An aircraft is created to fly in the sky while a ship is created to sail on the sea. A car on the other hand drives on land. All of the above are means of transportation, each carrying out their purpose according to the specific design of their creators.

You are on earth for a purpose:

- To pray for someone
- To open your ears and listen to someone's plight
- To share your gifts and talents
- To reach out to your local community
- To tend a home
- To champion a cause
- To respond to a particular need in the world
- To discover something

Since we did not create ourselves it is important to find out why we were created. For this understanding to be gained, we need to understand Divine Purpose.

What is Divine Purpose?

Divine purpose is the purpose set forth by God at creation. To understand our divine purpose we, as God's creation, must go back to where it first began. In the book of Genesis, we are told what the earth looked like before God began his work of creation. In Chapter 1 verse 2 it is said that the earth was without form and void and that total darkness covered the face of the earth. It was this darkness that spurred the work of creation. In the midst of this darkness, God said "Let there be light" and there was light. And so, creation unfolded one item after another till the sixth day.

Everything that God created He only had to speak and it manifested itself but when He was done creating the fauna and flora, the mountains and the seas and the firmament and rivers, He held a consultation with the Godhead for the very first time. He said, in the book of Genesis 1:26:

> "Let us make man in our image, after our likeness: and let them have dominion over the fish of the sea, and over the fowl of the air, and over the cattle, and over all the earth, and over every creeping thing that creepeth upon the earth."

The fact that God held a "consultation" with the Godhead before creating man shows us that Mankind was different and special from every other thing that He had created. Everything He created was a product of His imagination. Man is a "replica" of God. God created man after His own image after the likeness of the Godhead. That means that the qualities that the Godhead have are found in us. And the mandate we have as God's creation is to manifest the characteristics of the Godhead.

> "And God blessed them, and God said unto them, be fruitful, and multiply, and replenish the earth, and subdue it: and have dominion over the fish of the sea, and over the fowl of the air, and over every living thing that moveth upon the earth." (Gen 1:28).

The key word to note here is dominion. If we understand Gods original purpose for mankind it will also help us understand our unique purpose.

Let us take a quick look at the scope of the great entity called "Man" that God has created.

Mankind Is Created to Perform Feats

There are somewhere between 80 and 100 billion neurons (nerve cells) in the human brain. Your neural hard drive could store somewhere between 1,000 gigs and 2.5 million gigs equivalent to 125 million copies of a novel.

When put to the test, human beings have been known to perform mighty feats. Scientists call it 'hysterical strength' and there have been many reported stories of this happening, where an individual exercises "superhuman" strength in a time of great need.

A famous case of this happened in 1960 when Angela Carvallo's son was trapped under a car and upon waiting for help, she took the rescue into her own hands (literally) and lifted the car off him, allowing him to crawl out of harm's way.

Another example of incredible strength was from Charlotte Hefflemire in 2016. In similar circumstances, her dad became trapped under a leaking truck and through superhuman strength she managed to lift it off him and save him. These acts were fluke events as most people who achieve this are never able to replicate it but, still, it's a mystery as to how they did it in the first place.

God has so endowed man with wisdom, power, strength and intelligence that man has been to the moon, put skyscrapers in cities, built aircraft and even cured incurable diseases.

Man is truly a wonder.

The question then must be asked why it is that man does not seem to easily find his purpose on earth. Every day, men and women run helter-skelter, drudging to make ends meet and never quite getting the reason for their existence. In the end, they find themselves operating as square pegs in round holes. The result is frustration, bitterness and diseases related to worry, as most people are unhappy with what they do.

We will explore this further in the book.

A Few Questions Regarding Purpose

This book will raise more questions than provide answers.

This is deliberate and the reason for that is to shake you out of thoughtless acquiescence and get you thinking hard about your reason for passing this way.

Some of the questions we need to ask ourselves earlier on are as follows:

- Is purpose synonymous with prominence?
- Is purpose the same as having influence?
- Is purpose and wealth akin?
- Are purpose and religious faith inextricably linked?
- Can purpose change through life or is it cut in stone from the time we are born?

Purpose Vs Prominence

One of the things we would like to explore with you in the book is whether finding your purpose means you should be prominent. In other words, do you have to be well-known around the world to be considered a man or woman of purpose? Can it be said that Richard Branson the multi-billionaire with an impressive business portfolio spanning airlines, trains, holidays and financial products has found his calling and the gardener has not found hers simply because the one is a household name and the other an anonymous hand?

Purpose Vs Influence

Often when we talk about purpose, the inclination is to tag influential people as having found their purpose and the less influential as not having located the reason for their being.

Florence Nightingale came to prominence while serving as a manager of nurses trained by her during the Crimean War, where she organised the tending to wounded soldiers. She gave nursing a highly favourable reputation and became an icon of Victorian culture, especially in the persona of "The Lady with the Lamp" making rounds of wounded soldiers at night. Can it be said that Florence Nightingale found her purpose in life since she was famous and that the nurse tending to wounded soldiers in Iraq has not found hers?

Purpose Vs Wealth

It may be argued that the acquisition of great wealth is evidence of finding one's true purpose on earth. What would you say to that? Can it be said that Warren Buffet, the American business magnate, has found his calling as a business mogul while the social worker helping in the care home on a monthly salary have not found their purpose?

Purpose Vs Religious Faith

One of the most controversial exchanges today happen between Christians and non-Christians and in general between people of faith and those without a religion. Christians usually argue that anyone that has not given their life to Christ and confessed him openly as Lord cannot lay claim to their true purpose on earth. I once followed a TV interview between Larry King and Creflo Dollar. Dr Dollar told Larry in no uncertain terms that he had found his purpose in life and Larry had not. The one is a multi-accolade winning TV host. The other is renowned preacher. Can it be said that either has found their calling in what they do or shall we posit that Creflo Dollar has found the light and Larry still lives in darkness?

What Then is True Evidence of Purpose?

So, what then is the true gage to determine whether one has found their purpose? Thomas C Corley, a prominent writer and blogger on success, submits that:

> *"When you find your life's purpose, that thing you were meant to do, born to do, you know it. There is no doubt. You are 100% certain. If you have any doubts about whether you are pursuing a career that is your life's purpose, you are not. Doubts are life's way of informing you that you haven't found your main purpose in life".*

Grasping the characteristics of purpose can be extremely difficult especially when the person being considered has hidden talents or is functioning away from the limelight.

Bishop TD Jakes posits as follows:

> *"...Being good at something doesn't mean it's your calling... You must understand that the purpose is an underlying chemistry that makes you live your life. I was sitting on a speaker and I said, 'This speaker will bear the weight of my body. It will make a chair in a pinch'...but it was not designed to be a chair. I am not using it for its highest and best use. Many times, we are pushed into functioning in an area that is not our highest and best use because someone needed us to be something we were not created to be. If you're stuck on how to tell the difference between talent and purpose, look honestly at your best skills. So many times, you have a modicum of talent in an area, maybe just enough talent to appreciate people who are really called to that area. It doesn't mean that you need to necessarily go out and do that thing. However, if you're in a situation where your talents aren't being used to the maximum, it could be beneficial in the long run. You may start out doing something that was not 'the thing' that you were created to do. It may only be the thing that leads to the thing you were created to do. So, don't stop*

at where you are as if it were the destination, when in fact it may be the transportation that brings you into that thing you were created to do".

Now is the time for you to start pondering your own life. Are you happy with what you do? Do you feel satisfaction as you practice your vocation? If you are, there is a good chance that you have located your purpose. If not, fear not! The purpose of this book is to walk you through the process of locating the reason you came to earth.

Before we delve into the nitty-gritty, let us take a quick look at how God sees you in His grand scheme of life from creation till now.

CHAPTER 2

YOU ARE GOD'S ORIGINAL AND UNIQUE PURPOSE

"The purpose of life is a life of purpose."
Robert Bryne

THIS BOOK IS about finding our purpose and being we can be so that we can do the best that we can in line with God's original plan. Let us together explore the reason He made us in the first place.

Why Did God Create Us At All?

The question of why God created us has been tossed around by people, bible scholars and philosophers for centuries on end. But it is safe to say that God did not just create us out of boredom or out of curiosity or out of the thrill of a new experiment. The way God has related with man since creation is an indication of this purpose. Why did God make the earth and us along with it? He doesn't really need us, so why did he create anything?

Great question, and you're not the first to ask it. King David asked essentially the same thing:

> *"When I consider your heavens, the work of your fingers ... what is man that you are mindful of him, the son of man that you care for him?" (Psalm 8:3-4).*

Why did God make us? To answer that, we need to know three things:

First, and you mentioned this in your question, it wasn't because he needed us: *"The God who made the world and everything in it ... is not served by human hands, as if he needed anything"* (Acts 17:24-25).

And he didn't make us because he was lonely. Long before we were here, God already had "company" with his Son and the Holy Spirit, referred to in Genesis 1:26, *"Let us make man in our own image."*

And he didn't make us because he needed his ego fed. It's not like God made us to satisfy some craving to be worshiped. God is totally secure in who he is—without us.

Second, despite not needing us, God chose to create us anyway, out of his great love: *"I have loved you with an everlasting love"* *(Jeremiah 31:3)*. Yes, God loved us before he even created us. It's impossible to get our heads around that idea, but it's true; that's what "everlasting" love means.

God is love (1 John 4:8), and because of that love and his wonderful creativity, He made us so we can enjoy all that he is and all that He has done.

Third, God created us to fulfil his eternal plan. I could write pages and pages about this, but suffice it to say that God, in his infinite wisdom, chose to make us a part of his eternal plan.

What part do we play in this plan? Well, the Bible is full of instructions for how we should live our lives. But here are a few key verses to remember:

1. "Love the Lord your God with all your heart and with all your soul and with all your strength" (Deuteronomy 6:5).
2. "Love your neighbour as yourself" (Matthew 22:39).

3. "We are God's workmanship, created in Christ Jesus to do good works, which God prepared in advance for us to do" (Ephesians 2:10).

Fellowship With God

One key purpose of our existence on earth is fellowship with our Maker and Creator.

I will liken the Godhead to a couple who have gotten married. They have acquired everything thing that they need: a good house, cars, a good job, land, property and every living comfort that they desire except that the house is empty and there is no child to play in it. Imagine the beauty of the garden of Eden, with no one to admire it, tend it and enjoy the wondrous fruits that were being produced after every kind. We are told in Genesis that in the cool of the day God would come walking in the garden of Eden to check up on Adam and Eve.

> "And they heard the voice of the LORD God walking in the garden in the cool of the day: and Adam and his wife hid themselves from the presence of the LORD God amongst the trees of the garden". (Genesis 3:8).

We all have friends and or family and loved ones, school mates, work mates, neighbours or parents whom we check on from time to time. This is the same relationship that God had with Adam and Eve. He would come strolling in the Garden of Eden and chat with them to see how they were doing in the garden he had specially created for them. God created man to be in a relationship with him. A communion of sorts. A father and child bond.

Fellowship with God is such a big thing that it should be a priority because through fellowship with Him, we tend to be like Him and show mercy and forgiveness to others.

We can become distracted from our mission, and consider the physical activities of ministry (even though they are necessary) so important that we have little if any time for fellowship with God. When we are busily engaged in hectic activity on God's behalf (at least at the time it seems that we are engaged in God's business) we can forget what Jesus said in Matthew 23:23: "Woe to you, teachers of the law and Pharisees, you hypocrites. You give a tenth of your spices – mint, dill and cummin. But you have neglected the important matters of the law – justice, mercy and faithfulness. You should have practiced the latter, without neglecting the former."

That is why the fall of man was an archetypical tragedy, an astounding stab in the back of God that would take many centuries to repair.

Dominion Over All Things

It is important to note that even though God created all the animals and birds, He did not give a name to any single animal. It is only after Adam was created that he brought them to Adam to give them names. The first way that Adam exercised his dominion was by naming all the animals that God had created.

> *"And out of the ground the* LORD *God formed every beast of the field, and every fowl of the air; and brought them unto Adam to see what he would call them: and whatsoever Adam called every living creature, that was the name thereof.*

> *And Adam gave names to all cattle, and to the fowl of the air, and to every beast of the field; but for Adam there was not found an help meet for him." (Genesis 2:19-20).*

Here we see Adam working in partnership with God in naming all the animals that God had created. Man was created to live in harmony with its creator, have fellowship with him and have dominion over all that God had created. The bible tells us that God commanded Adam and Eve to have dominion over everything he had created.

> *"And God blessed them, and God said unto them, Be fruitful, and multiply, and replenish the earth, and subdue it: and have dominion over the fish of the sea, and over the fowl of the air, and over every living thing that moves upon the earth." (Genesis 1:28).*

Understanding Dominion

Dominion is derived from the Latin word *"dominium"* from *"dominus"* which means "Lord or Master". To have dominion over something, somebody or territory, means to have and exercise complete control over them. This means that God created Man to be Lord and Master over everything He had created. God wanted man to subdue the earth and be in total control of everything in it. As man answereth to God so all creation was supposed to answer to man.

Synonyms of dominion include ascendancy, dominance, domination, superiority, predominance, pre-eminence, hegemony, authority, mastery, control, command, direction, power, sway, rule, government, jurisdiction, sovereignty, lordship, over lordship. This was man's assignment to have authority over, direct, command and hold sway over every created thing. This is the position of glory from which man fell.

I want to use the teacher student analogy to further explain dominion. A teacher is given authority to not only teach but exercise control, discipline and keep his students in line always. Imagine you went into a class and there were students standing on tables, some chatting away, some on their phones others on the floor playing while the teacher sat at his desk and said or did nothing to restore order in the classroom. The teachers lack of control has given birth to total classroom anarchy the type that needs the intervention of a discipline master or principal to bring things back under control.

Your Highest Self

We have already seen how God created us as His special project and gave us the power to become his sons and do exploits. If we remind ourselves of this fact all the time, we cannot stop looking for our purpose, the one thing we were created to do. When we locate that purpose, we begin to operate from the divine perspective and there is no stopping us.

As we will see later in Chapter 8, great men and women of our time do not have two brains of four eyes; they are ordinary mortals who have tapped into the mind of God for them and have paid the price to carry out their purpose on earth.

Thankfully, this ability to tap into the mind of God is available to everyone. There's a level of awareness available to you that you are perhaps not used to. It stretches upward and goes beyond the ordinary level of consciousness that you're most familiar with. At this higher plane of living, which you and every human being who has ever lived can access as you choose, manifesting your dreams is not only a possibility—it is guaranteed. By entering that dimension, you have much more control over what comes into your life than you might have imagined. I've seen from personal experience how virtually every wish or desire I've focused on has transformed from a mere thought into a physical fact. My point here is that manifestation is real and that it occurs when you make a firm decision to change your perception about who you are and what is possible for you to accomplish within this part of the journey of creation called your life.

I hereby call on you to receive to a bold new idea about yourself. It's bold because ever since your mother gave birth to you, you've been put under environmental influences created to help you be content with living a "normal life" at the level of ordinary consciousness, which generally means accepting whatever life hands you. In many ways you've been programmed to believe that you do not possess the knowledge or ability to manifest the birth of your wishes and desires.

Let me say it now with all the boldness I can muster. There's a level of being that you can opt to live at, in which you can, if you are willing to change your conception of yourself as an ordinary entity, find yourself fulfilling any and all wishes that you have set for yourself. It starts with changing your concept of yourself.

I would like to offer a few words on the two concepts of ordinary and extraordinary.

Ordinary is, well, so ordinary. It means that you do all of the things that your culture and your family have programmed you to do. It implies that you fit in, study hard, follow the law, take care of your duties, fill out the forms, pay your taxes, get employment, and do what every law-abiding citizen does; and then you retire, play with your grandchildren, and then you die. I want to emphasize that there is absolutely nothing wrong with this at all—it is perfectly fine—but if it were completely acceptable for you, you wouldn't be reading this book.

Extraordinary contains most of ordinary, since we all live in the same physical world. There will be forms to complete, rules that call for our obedience, bills to settle, and family duties to fulfil. However, the extraordinary mindset is associated with your soul, that invisible, limitless energy that looks out from behind your eyes and has very different perceptions from your ordinary self. What your soul craves above everything else, is not more knowledge. It is not interested in comparing things, nor winning, nor light, nor ownership, nor even happiness. What your soul desires is more room, more space, and immensity, and the one thing it needs more than anything else is to be free to grow, to reach out and to embrace the limitless. The simple reason for this is that your soul is infinity itself. It has no restrictions or limitations—it does not like being hemmed in—and when you try to restrict it with rules and obligations, it is miserable.

Your invisible self is extraordinary because it is a piece of the universal soul, which is infinite. The part of you that knows you have greatness within you, and is moved by the idea of you expanding and removing any and all limitations, is what I am talking about here. This is your new concept of self, one that is driven by your soul.

If you would like to become a person who has the capacity to have all of your dreams come true, you would need to move to that higher plane of existence where you are a co-creator of your life. This means that you have to begin what is often thought of as being the difficult task of changing your concept of yourself.

Remember that your concept of yourself is everything that you believe to be true about your inner and outer self. Those beliefs have created the life you're now living—at what I call an ordinary level of awareness. To move into the extraordinary space that I'm writing about requires you to change what you believe is true. *A higher concept of yourself involves taking on new truths and shedding your old views of what you can achieve.* This is the only way you can achieve your desires. You must begin by replacing your old set of truths with a belief in the existence of a higher self within you. This is akin to doing a somersault and landing in a new reality—a reality in which all things are possible.

The big question then is this? Why, despite the mandate that God gave us at creation, do we not take charge of our lives, find our purpose and perform great feats? A lot of us wake up each day, line up on the motorway to do a job we do not like. After years of toil, we become knackered and life has passed us by. In our later years, we realise that we missed the purpose train. Then we start frantically trying to catch up.

The time to start is now! Now is the time to reconnect with the God that created you and draw power to do great things. Daniel

11:32 says *"the people that do know their God shall be strong, and do exploits"*. Arise from your slumber today and start carrying out your assignment. Wake up from your stupor and start doing what you came here to do. When your job here on earth is done, you do not want to take a negative report to your Maker. You want Him to welcome you and say, "well done faithful servant"!

Before you embark on the journey of self-discovery, I would like us to look at some banana peelings on the journey that may try to trip you and rob you of your divine purpose.

That would be the thrust of Chapter 3.

CHAPTER 3

HINDRANCES TO DISCOVERING YOUR PURPOSE

"A life without a purpose is a life without a destination.
Like a boat adrift on the ocean, there is no telling
where you might end up". Dr Jim White

IN CHAPTER 2 we saw how man was created great from the very beginning of time. We saw that man has the ability to dominate the planet and even other planets. We read how Man has access to limitless abilities.

In this chapter, we will look at some obstacles that may stand in the way of Man's quest for, and fulfilment of, his purpose. Please bear in mind that these obstacles are not highlighted to discourage you in your quest for God's plan; they are meant to keep you alert so that you may recognise and overcome them.

Man's Fall from Grace

The fall from grace is a term used idiomatically to refer to how Adam and Eve transitioned from a state of innocent obedience to God their creator to a state of guilty disobedience. All through Genesis chapter one we see a state of harmony where God is busy with creation: giving order to a formless earth. Then we move on to chapter 2 where God creates man to be overseer to all created things. We see man's obedience and innocent fellowship with his maker and how the two work together in fulfilling creation's purpose. God freely gave man the right to partake of everything he had created with only one exception;

> And the LORD God commanded the man, saying, of every tree of the garden thou mayest freely eat: But of the tree of the knowledge of good and evil, thou shalt not eat of it: for in the day that thou eats thereof thou shalt surely die". (Gen 2: 16-17).

The only condition of continual fellowship with God was that Adam and Eve should keep away from the tree of the knowledge of good and evil. On mount Sinai, the Israelites were given 10 commandments but in the beginning Adam and Eve only had one commandment and it was the failure to adhere to this one injunction that has plunged mankind into restlessness. Through this one act of disobedience sin entered the world and was passed down to all generations. Adam having lost this position has plunged man into an endless quest to regain this position.

The immediate consequence of Adams sin of disobedience towards God was prompt banishment from the garden of Eden where he had enjoyed communion with his maker.

> "Therefore, the LORD God sent him forth from the garden of Eden, to till the ground from whence he was taken. So, he drove out the man; and he placed at the east of the garden of Eden Cherubims, and a flaming sword which turned every way, to keep the way of the tree of life." (Gen 3: 23-24).

Every entity involved in this act of disobedience had some form of punishment to endure. Adam because he had harkened unto the voice of his wife and eaten of the fruit of the tree of the knowledge of good and evil, he was condemned to hard labour.

> And unto Adam he said, Because thou hast hearkened unto the voice of thy wife, and hast eaten of the tree, of which I commanded thee, saying, Thou shalt not eat of it: cursed is the ground for thy sake; in sorrow shalt thou eat of it all the

days of thy life; Thorns also and thistles shall it bring forth to thee; and thou shalt eat the herb of the field; In the sweat of thy face shalt thou eat bread, till thou return unto the ground; for out of it was thou taken: for dust thou art, and unto dust shalt thou return. (Genesis 3:17-19).

Not only was Adam driven away from the presence and fellowship with God, he was condemned to eating bread out of the sweat of his forehead: which signifies manual labour. From the abundance that was readily available in the garden of Eden, Adam now had to till the ground and eat from his sweat.

Eve was the supreme culprit in that she took the fruit from the serpent and gave it to her husband to eat, causing him to disobey the commandment which God gave to Adam. In Genesis chapter 1 when God blessed Adam and Eve and commanded them to be fruitful and multiply and replenish the earth, there was no mention of pain in childbirth. But when they disobeyed God a curse was spoken out to Eve:

"And I will put enmity between thee and the woman, and between thy seed and her seed; it shall bruise thy head, and thou shalt bruise his heel. Unto the woman he said, I will greatly multiply thy sorrow and thy conception; in sorrow thou shalt bring forth children; and thy desire shall be to thy husband, and he shall rule over thee." (Genesis 3: 15-16).

Not only Adam and Eve were cursed; the serpent also got a dealing of the Lords anger at this this great betrayal which had taken place in the garden.

"And the LORD God said unto the serpent, because thou hast done this, thou art cursed above all cattle, and above every beast of the field; upon thy belly shalt thou go, and dust shalt thou eat all the days of thy life:" (Genesis 3:14).

The fall of Man has had a huge impact on the way we live our lives today and given rise to some major hindrances in the quest for our divine purpose.

The Pressures of Life

Since the fall of Man in the garden of Eden, man has taken on the adamic nature and surrendered to the pressures of life. Studies have shown that fully 97% of the world's population has no goals and works for the 3% who do. Life has become a long and painful process of waking up early, finding oneself to work, putting in long hours, collecting a meagre pay cheque at the end of the month and starting all over again. Then there are taxes, utility bills, medical bills, the needs of family and relatives and the list goes on.

As a result of these pressures, Man is finding it difficult to pause and think of the purpose for which he was created. How can a factory worker who works a 12-hour shift every day stop and think of the reason why they came to earth? The consequence of drudgery is that the quest for purpose is soon forgotten.

However, the pursuit of one's purpose may sometimes mean that one has to forgo subsistence or acquire knowledge that can enable one to set aside quality time to work on their vision.

Fear of Starting All Over Again

One of the greatest hindrances to finding and fulfilling one's purpose on earth is the fear of starting all over again. God speaks to His children all the time and a lot of us know that we are not fulfilling our purpose on earth. Some of us are supposed to be preaching but we are bus drivers; some of us are supposed to be engineers but we are preaching; some of us are supposed to be medical doctors but we are stock brokers. Finding yourself in a dilemma as you navigate through life is not a problem. The real problem is refusing to dismantle what we have built so far and starting all over again.

TD Jakes captures that dilemma when he says:

> *"You may start out doing something that was not 'the thing' that you were created to do. It may only be the thing that leads to the thing you were created to do. So, don't stop at where you are as if it were the destination, when in fact in reality it may be the transportation that brings you into that thing you were created to do."*

Man is a creature of habit and once a pattern is set, it is hard to break it.

However, taking a radical step and moving toward your purpose may be necessary so that you do not look back and regret not having fulfilled God's plan for your life.

Most Christians love Ron Kenoly's music but few know that he was not a gospel musician when he started. Ron made a U-turn from roc music to gospel music when he was nearly 50 years old. His story is so compelling that I take the liberty of telling it at length here.

Ron is one of the world's leading worship leaders. Very few people who enjoy his music know that he began as a rock musician. There is nothing wrong with rock music. But Ron was never created by God to be a rock star. After high school, Ron did a three-year stretch in the Air Force from 1965 to 1968. It was while in the service that he met and married his wife, Tavita, and where he joined his first real band, called the *Mellow Fellows*. He soon became a sought-after nightclub performer, and released nine singles on four major labels. As his secular music career took off, Ron's family life began to suffer. Separated several times and on the edge of divorce, Ron admits that he had made his career his god, and left his wife and three children on the periphery of his life. "My wife rededicated her life to the Lord in 1975 and began praying for the healing of our family," says Ron. "I began to realize the goodness of God because I could see the changes He was making in her life, and I could see that while I never lost respect for God, I had never had a strong spiritual life.

That's when the lights began to come on for me, because I was beginning to see all the things about Jesus that before I had only heard. I wanted the joy that she had found."

Ron recommitted his life to Christ that same year, remaining in Los Angeles and secular music for another year-and-a-half to fulfil lingering contractual commitments. When he left LA, he relocated with his family to Oakland, California, and completed a degree in music at Alameda College.

"From 1976 to 1978, while I was in school, I just surrendered my life to the Lord, allowing Him to do some character building in me," says Ron. "I had to learn to be a husband and a father, and I had to learn how to relate to God as a Father. I still sang, but only every Sunday in the bass section of Bethel Missionary Baptist Church." Ron taught music and physical education at Alameda from 1978 to 1982, and though he found a sense of peace in turning his life over to the Lord and His will, the fire to sing still burned within him.

In 1978, Ron decided his next logical move would be to land a Christian record deal, but after four years of almost total unresponsiveness from the Christian industry he became disheartened. Ron's despondency was heightened by the fact that throughout that time, secular labels continued to call him, expressing interest in rekindling old relationships. By 1982 it seemed to Ron as if the world wanted him, but Christianity was somehow not interested.

One evening in the summer of 1982, Ron sat alone in his church for hours, playing, singing, praying, worshipping, and laying his burdens before the Lord. "From that night on, the record companies ceased to matter," says Ron. "The Lord had met me and shown me so much that I felt I had gone beyond what any company could offer me. Acceptance and rejection didn't matter anymore because all I knew was that I had been with God."

Ron left the church that night with nothing but a desire to worship and praise God, and to lead others in doing the same. Soon, word of Ron's musical talents began to spread around the Oakland area, and he found himself invited to lead praise and worship at numerous churches.

"I didn't even think of myself as a praise and worship leader", Ron says. "All I knew was I would go and sing my songs and something special would happen". In 1983, Kenoly produced his custom-made album, "You Ought to Listen to This." He sold the album wherever he sang. Soon, offers to lead praise and worship came flooding in from churches in the area. In 1985, Pastor Dick Bernal, Founder of the Jubilee Christian Centre in San Jose, CA, invited Kenoly to be the church's Minister of Music. Shortly after, Don Moen of Integrity Music heard about Kenoly's music. In 1991, Integrity released Kenoly's first gospel album, "Jesus is Alive", which quickly became a surprise hit, followed by "Lift Him Up," "God is Able," "Sing Out," "Welcome Home," "High Places," "Majesty" and "We Offer Praises".

With all 8 albums, Kenoly sold more than 4 million copies. Two albums received gold record sale status and three live videos went gold. Kenoly received 19 GMA Dove Award nominations and won one Dove Award for "Welcome Home." "Every season of my life has had its own lessons. I think that's true for all of us. You never learn persistence until you have something you really want. You never learn faith until you have trials to test who you are and what you believe."

Thank God that Ron made the decision to start all over again and find his divine purpose in life. Millions of people around the world would have missed out on his ministry.

Perhaps God's voice is telling you exactly what you need to do to fulfil your divine purpose. It does not matter how far you have gone with your current assignment. Set the car in reverse, go back and start your new assignment. When you do so, you will flourish in it and the world will be a better place because you came.

Low Self-Esteem

One of the reasons why people do not pursue their divine purpose is the fact that they have a very low opinion of themselves.

Your self-esteem determines how high you can rise in life. Dr Maxwell Maltz, in his great book *The New Psycho-Cybernetics*, says "You can never perform higher or lower than your self-esteem". The subject of self-esteem is so important that you should dedicate plenty of time to its study. Go to a mirror right now and look at yourself. What do you see? A Christian struggling with debts? A "humble" woman just getting by? A world mover and shaker? An inspiring author? You cannot be more or less than what you see in that mirror. You can pray till thy kingdom come, but nothing will change if you do not change your conception of self.

It was a high self-esteem that pushed Barack Obama, a rookie politician, to shoot for the greatest presidency on earth and get it. Proverbs 23:7 says: "As a man thinketh in his heart, so is he".

My challenge to you today is this. If you have discovered what your divine purpose is, do not do a Moses and complain that you are a stutterer. Here was a man that God himself commanded to go out and set His people free. He looked at his own personal frailties and tried to wriggle himself out of the assignment, his divine purpose. In Exodus 4:10 he moaned:

> "... O my Lord, I am not eloquent, neither heretofore, nor since thou hast spoken unto thy servant: but I am slow of speech, and of a slow tongue".

When God is with you, you are twice the woman or the man. All your frailties become assets and you will fulfil your divine purpose in Jesus' Name!

Living Life Without Goals

John Barrymore says, "without goals, vision or purpose, we are susceptible to depression, boredom or dissipation of time and energy".

It's been said that a life without goals is like a race with no finish line; you're just running to nowhere.

We all set goals throughout our days, weeks and months both consciously and more oftentimes automatically. These goals help us to determine the level of success that we feel we have achieved in life. Now there are plenty of people who are ambitious and plan to "rule the world" one day and many more that get through life without consciously setting goals. Regardless of which category you fall into, it's important to realize the opportunities that can materialize through goal setting and why you should be taking conscious (and massive) action on them.

Setting clearly defined goals will help you to be more focused on the things that are important to your life's objectives and deter you from time-wasting activities. Once you have achieved a goal or milestone, you can attach meaning to your deep desires and create a sense of purpose. This will ultimately fuel your passion and keep you motivated in the long term. Being clear on your goals will help you to avoid activities that may seem urgent but are irrelevant and allow you to focus on tasks that are important. This will stop you from procrastinating and feeling overwhelmed with responsibilities and allow you to free up additional time to work on your divine purpose.

Lack of Tenacity

Knowing your divine purpose is one thing. Starting to work on it is another thing. Staying with it until it is accomplished is yet another. Quick surrender has undone many visionaries in times past and continues to unravel people of vision in our time.

God is aware that every purpose He puts in us has a gestation period. That is why He gave us a staff to hold when we feel weary:

> *"Write the vision, and make it plain upon tables, that he may run that readeth it. For the vision is yet for an appointed time, but at the end it shall speak, and not lie: though it tarry, wait for it; because it will surely come, it will not tarry". (Habakkuk 2:2-3).*

Our God encourages us to wait for it even if it seems to tarry. The old saying goes that "pressure makes diamonds". In order for you to fulfil your divine purpose, you need to be tenacious. You need to be able to pass through several small and large failures and establish yourself as the true owner of that purpose. The computer expert is the greatest computer failure. The reason she is able to troubleshoot every problem you face is because she has faced and overcome them.

Do not be one of those that looks back and says, "I wish I had stayed with that dream for 5 years". Hold on to your purpose till you accomplish it.

Despite Man's fall from grace and the negative outcomes of that fall outlined in this chapter, we are set free to live out our divine purpose and enjoy a life of abundance through the redemptive power of Jesus Christ.

That will be the object of our next chapter.

CHAPTER 4

GOD'S PLAN OF REDEMPTION THROUGH CHRIST

"I am come that they might have life, and that they might have *it* more abundantly". John 10:10

IN CHAPTER 3, we looked at some factors hindering Man's ability to find and fulfil his divine purpose, chief among which was Man's fall from grace. In this chapter, we announce the Good News that all is not lost. God sent His only begotten Son Jesus to die on the cross for our sins and through the great sacrifice, He has made us whole again.

Let us look at the main tenets of this redemptive power and how it impacts on our ability to find and fulfil our divine purpose.

God's Heart Cry

> "The Lord is not slack concerning his promise, as some men count slackness; but is longsuffering to us-ward, not willing that any should perish, but that all should come to repentance". (2 Peter 3:9).

As earthly beings, we sometimes feel that when a child goes away from home either as punishment for bad behaviour or out of the stubbornness of their heart as some children do, that only the child feels the pain of separation. Dislocation from the family tree is a pain that is felt by both child and parent. None of us should underestimate the pain and emptiness that God felt from being separated from man whom He had so lovingly created. That is why he came to the garden in the First place in the cool of the day to check on Adam and Eve. He knew they had disobeyed Him but he still came to chat with them. God weeps for banished creation and desires that they should return to Him.

> "Then saith he unto his disciples, The harvest truly is plenteous, but the labourers are few; Pray ye therefore the Lord of the harvest, that he will send forth labourers into his harvest." (Mathew 9:38-39).

The Seed of the woman referred to Christ who will later come to save mankind. God's cry is two-fold. His first cry is for His fallen sons and daughter to be reconciled to Him. His second cry is that there are so many more souls wanting to find this path back to Him, than there are labourers to help in this task.

The Great Atonement

When Adam and Eve sinned, God performed the first act of atonement by clothing them with a coat made out of the skin of an animal. Before the fall of man Adam and his wife Eve had roamed about naked in the garden of Eden. But when they sinned, they realised they were naked and used fig leaves to cover themselves in shame. God had to provide a covering for them and to do this an innocent animal had to be killed for the sole purpose of covering their nakedness.

The killing of an animal implies the shedding of blood. This is a foreshadowing of what was going to happen to Christ on the cross of Calvary. Although Adam and Eve had sinned against God and he banished them from the Garden of Eden, He put in place a "scheme" where the seed of the woman will bruise the head of the serpent. Like every good father though His children had sinned against Him, He was willing to make a way for His estranged children to be reconciled to Himself.

All of Man's existence according to the Christian world view is to find the link back to its maker through the redemption that is purchased by the blood of Christ on the cross of Calvary, live in the body of Christ while hear on earth displaying Gods dominion, helping in the divine mandate of reconciling people back to God through Evangelism and finally going back to be with God in the Garden of Eden.

> *"And he made known to us the mystery of his will according to his good pleasure, which he purposed in Christ, to be put into effect when the times will have reached their fulfilment – to bring all things in heaven and on earth together under one head, even Christ" (Ephesians 1:9-10).*

This threefold task of finding our way to God, tending the flock of God and helping other lost sheep find their way home is the embodiment of the Divine purpose of God for all mankind. This is what I call Gods Heart cry.

Our duty then is to find out which purpose we can fulfil in this great commission.

The Benefits of Redemption

On the cross, Jesus took upon Himself the curses due to us by our disobedience so that, in turn, we might enter into the blessings Jesus earned by His obedience. These blessings cover the whole area of the kingdom of light. The blessings we receive are three-pronged – spiritual, physical and material.

Spiritual Benefits

What are the blessings in the spiritual realm that result from obedience? Of course, there are countless blessings. But I believe they can be summed up in one short and beautiful word: peace.

When Isaiah wrote about the exchange that took place when Jesus died on the cross, he said this, *"The punishment that brought us peace was upon him"* (Isaiah 53:5). Jesus endured the judgment and the punishment due to our sin and disobedience that we might be reconciled with God. As a result of being reconciled with God, we can be delivered from inner agony, torment, confusion and frustration. We can know the reality of a deep, settled, inward peace.

Let's look at two other Scriptures in the New Testament that speak of this peace.

> *"Therefore, having been justified by faith, we have peace with God through our Lord Jesus Christ"*. (Romans 5:1).

> *"And the peace of God, which transcends all understanding, will guard your hearts and your minds in Christ Jesus"*. (Philippians 4:7).

What beautiful words! No longer are we guilty. No longer do we fear that somehow; we are not pleasing God. We have peace with God. This beautiful verse in Philippians 4 describes the experiential results within us. The peace of God will guard our hearts and minds in our contemporary civilization.

In its Hebrew form, the word 'peace' means more than just the absence of conflict. It means wholeness or well-being. This type of peace begins in the inner man, but it leads to total well-being. It affects every area of our lives. John 14:27 says, "Peace I leave with you, my peace I give unto you: not as the world giveth, give I unto you. Let not your heart be troubled, neither let it be afraid".

Physical Benefits

Let's look now at the physical blessings that were purchased for us by Jesus. Isaiah 53:4–5: says:

"Surely, He took our infirmities and carried our sorrows yet we considered him stricken by God, smitten by him, and afflicted. But He was pierced for our transgressions, he was crushed for our iniquities; the punishment that brought us peace was upon him, and by his wounds we are healed".

Jesus took the physical consequences of disobedience that we might in turn have healing. We see this in that phrase at the end of verse 5, *"By his wounds we are healed."* More literally in Hebrew it says, "By his wounds it was healed for us." Or we could perhaps say, "by his wounds healing was obtained for us." Healing was made our inheritance through the wounds that Jesus bore on His body.

The next part of this passage is quoted in the New Testament in Matthew's gospel, describing the ministry of Jesus in healing the sick and casting out evil spirits. This is what it says:

"When evening came, they brought to Him many who were demon-possessed; and He cast out the spirits with a word, and healed all who were ill. This was to fulfill what was spoken through Isaiah the prophet: "He Himself took our infirmities and carried away our diseases." (Matthew 8:16–17).

Matthew had no doubt who was referred to in Isaiah 53. He applied it to Jesus. Notice also that Matthew (who was a Jew and understood Hebrew), had no doubt that the application of those verses in Isaiah 53 was physical. It was the physical healing of the sick that was the fulfilment of the prophecy given in Isaiah. Jesus says in answering His critics for healing a man on the Sabbath:

"If a man receives circumcision on the Sabbath so that the Law of Moses may not be broken, are you angry with Me because I made an entire man well on the Sabbath?" (John 7:23).

Jesus makes the entire man well. Every area of human being and human personality can be healed through Jesus.

Notice too what Peter said after the healing of the lame man at the Beautiful Gate in Acts 3:16. This is how he explained the healing: "By faith in the name of Jesus, this man whom you see and know was made strong. It is Jesus' Name and the faith that comes through him that has given this complete healing to him, as you all can see".

What is the result? "Complete healing." Jesus said, "I've made an entire man well." That is the physical outworking of the redemption provided for us by Jesus. We are grateful for the work of physicians, psychiatrists and others. But there is only one person in the universe who can say, "I make an entire man well! I can deal with all his problems: spiritual, mental, emotional, physical." Who is that Person? The Lord Jesus Christ.

As we contact Jesus by faith on the basis of His redemption, the same results that took place and are recorded in the New Testament are available to you and me today through faith in Jesus.

Material Benefits

One of the greatest benefits of redemption is the conference of material benefits. Wealth, riches and abundance are our portion in Christ. Deuteronomy 8:18 says:

> *"But thou shalt remember the LORD thy God: for it is he that giveth thee power to get wealth, that he may establish his covenant which he swore unto thy fathers, as it is this day".*

3 John 1 verse 2 says: *"Beloved, I wish above all things that thou mayest prosper and be in health, even as thy soul prospereth".*

When Jesus was on the cross, He was hungry, He was thirsty, He was naked, and He was in want of all things. Why? It had to be this way because He exhausted the poverty curse on our behalf. He completely took the curse away once and for all so that you and I, redeemed believers through the blood of Jesus, might not have to endure that yoke of iron—that poverty curse.

This exchange is clearly summed up in the New Testament. In 2 Corinthians, we get the two aspects of the exchange in the material realm. Paul says:

> *"For you know the grace of our Lord Jesus Christ, that though He was rich, yet for your sake He became poor, so that you through His poverty might become rich".* (2 Corinthians 8:9). *"And God is able to make all grace abound to you, so that always having all sufficiency in everything, you may have abundance for every good deed".* (2 Corinthians 9:8).

That is the great exchange! Jesus took our poverty on the cross that we in turn might have access to His wealth and to His abundance. It is through grace. Grace comes only through Jesus Christ. Grace cannot be earned. Grace is appropriated only by faith.

In the original Greek, that statement in 2 Corinthians 9:8 is amazing. The word 'abound' occurs twice, and the word 'all' occurs five times! This is what Jesus has obtained for us. He exhausted the poverty curse that we might inherit the blessings.

The blessings in all three areas obtained for us by Jesus—the spiritual, the physical and the material—are summed up in that beautiful verse of the third epistle of John, verse 2, where John says:

> *"Beloved, I wish above all things that thou mayest prosper and be in health, even as thy soul prospereth".*

That is the will of God. That is your inheritance as a believer in Jesus Christ.

Redemption Empowers You To Fulfil Your Divine Purpose

Now we know that redemption has taken away the curse that was upon us before. Redemption has given us health, wealth and a sound mind. Redemption has empowered us to carry out our purpose on earth. Redemption has given us all the necessary resources required to fulfil our calling. You have no more excuse! Armed with this realisation that heaven is behind you all the way, it is time to take up your mantle and follow in the footsteps of our Lord and Saviour Jesus Christ. In the next chapter, we will meet some champions of divine purpose and study how they found direction.

Come along with me.

PART 2

HOW TO FIND YOUR DIVINE PURPOSE

CHAPTER 5

HOW PEOPLE FIND THEIR PURPOSE IN LIFE

"Purpose is an underlying chemistry that makes you live your life". Bishop TD Jakes

FINDING YOUR PURPOSE in life can be a very challenging exercise if we do not know what we are doing. But you would agree with me that finding and living out our purpose in life is centrifugal to our existence. We were not born to just come and exist in this world float around and finally die without ever having found any real meaning in our life. We need to do soul searching. Who am I? Where do I come from? What am I doing here? What is my purpose? Where am I heading to? This is a very important aspect of life. How to know one's purpose is not just a Game that we can play. We cannot flip a coin heads or tails to find that out neither can we pull ballots randomly out of a hat to find our divine purpose. Any quest must be the result of serious soul searching and thought. How do we go about finding our purpose or life assignment?

It would seem from our study that there are two major ways of discovering one's divine purpose – predestination and deliberate creation.

Finding Purpose Through Predestination

Predestination supposes that you are born with a blueprint that God has tagged you with so that you grow up being a manifestation of the blueprint.

> Jeremiah 1:5 says, "Before I formed thee in the belly, I knew thee; and before thou come forth out of the womb, I sanctified thee, and I ordained thee a prophet unto the nations".

This verse seems to lend credence to our hypothesis that God carves out our destiny at birth. Your life began as a brilliant thought in God's mind. Your purpose, therefore, is the awakening to that thought. This perception of the meaning of divine purpose supposes that *you* don't find purpose; purpose finds you. Purpose conceived you. It was the catalyst for your birth. It is not the destination but an awareness. And that awareness determines the destinations and locations. It's not about where you go but Who guides you.

In the case of predestination, God seems to intervene directly to establish the person in the purpose. In other words, it is purpose by commandment.

Let us look at some examples.

Mary and The Nativity Experience

When Mary was espoused to be married to Joseph the carpenter, an angel of the Lord appeared to her. Many people have given accounts of angelic visitations and visions when faced with life changing decisions, turning points or important destiny signposts. For someone going to fulfil a world-changing decision like the birth of the Saviour of the world, it took an angelic visitation to deliver the message to Mary. What is also important to note here is that we are not told that she was sitting on a hill in a white robe, hands lifted in the air kneeling but that it happened during the day while she was going about her normal chores. Sometimes people assume that to get a divine instruction they must be doing something "outrageously" spiritual for that to happen.

Here is how the angel of the Lord dropped the news to her in Luke 1: 31-33:

> *"And, behold, thou shalt conceive in thy womb, and bring forth a son, and shalt call his name Jesus. He shall be great, and shall be called the Son of the Highest: and the Lord God shall give unto him the throne of his father David: And he shall reign over the house of Jacob for ever; and of his kingdom there shall be no end".*

Mary did not have to figure out her divine purpose of being the forbear of the Messiah. It was proclaimed from above.

Saul and The Damascus Experience

Paul was a Jew to the core. He was well-schooled in the teachings of the law and in his own eyes, and followed the teachings of the law to the best of his ability. He was zealous in the pursuit of his religion and carried out his duties faithfully by persecuting Christians who had come up with this new religion that was threatening to destabilize the status quo.

Many Christian scholars have purported that apart from the birth, death and resurrection of Jesus Christ and maybe the bringing to life of Lazarus, the conversion of Saul of Tarsus is the most dramatic event in the bible. As Saul was yet on another mission to Damascus to capture Christians, and bring them to Jerusalem for torture, the Lord met Him in a most dramatic way.

> *"And as he journeyed, he came near Damascus: and suddenly there shined round about him a light from heaven: And he fell to the earth, and heard a voice saying unto him, Saul, Saul, why persecutes thou me? And he said, Who art thou,*

*Lord? And the Lord said, I am Jesus whom thou persecutes:
it is hard for thee to kick against the pricks." (Acts 9:3-5).*

This is the most dramatic conversion recorded in the bible. When Jesus was putting together the apostles, He walked on the shores of the Sea of Galilee and seeing fishermen He told them simply, *"Follow me and I will make you fishers of men"* and they left their nets and followed Christ. But for Paul it took many different tactics. First of all, there was a geological intervention. As he journeyed on his way to Damascus, suddenly there shone a light from Heaven the sheer intensity of which made him fall unto the ground. A voice spoke to him, addressing him directly: *"Saul, Saul, Saul, why persecutes thou me?"* This was the beginning of Saul's brush with Christianity and his subsequent commissioning to the gentiles. Apart from that he was struck with blindness and led by the hand to Damascus. God also visited Ananias and asked him to go and pray for the newly converted Paul, telling Ananias explicitly what Paul's mission and purpose would be. Pauls purpose was to carry the gospel to the gentiles and he did it with the same zeal with which he had persecuted the Christians at the time, enduring many perils himself. Paul regained his sight, was filled with the holy ghost and became the greatest evangelist of all time. Paul alone is responsible for writing 12 books of the New Testament and became very influential in the spreading of Christianity to Europe and other parts of the world. The one thing that stands out about Paul is the fact that despite his trials and tribulations he is one of the few who not only found but fulfilled their purpose on earth.

"I have fought a good fight, I have finished my course, I have kept the faith:

Henceforth there is laid up for me a crown of righteousness, which the Lord, the righteous judge, shall give me at that day: and not to me only, but unto all them also that love his appearing." 2 Tim 4:7-8.

Paul is therefore one more example of a person who was given their purpose by a divine edict. He was made an oracle for God by a Godly arrest.

It is very satisfying to be able to look at the end of your life and be confident enough to say while you lived, you found out what it was that you were supposed to be doing, and did it to the best of your ability all the days of your life. It would be great if we could all receive such dramatic calls to service but it won't be like that for everybody.

Another biblical figure who received such a call was Moses.

Moses and The Burning Bush Experience

Moses was saved by Pharaoh's daughter in a time of political turmoil. The Israelites had been in slavery for a very long time in Egypt. Both men and women were accustomed to forced manual labour. It was so tough that the Hebrew women would hide their pregnancy and continue working. At every opportunity, the Egyptians increased the workload of the Hebrew slaves but this still did not slow them down. The birth rate among the Hebrews was also very high, so Pharaoh ordered that all new-born male children killed. He feared that if the slave population continued to increase in the event of an uprising, the men could constitute an army and fight against Egypt. So, killing boys would greatly reduce their military might and assure Egypt of continued dominance over Israel.

The birth of Moses was hidden but after three months, his mother could hide him no more. So, she put him in a basket and hid him in the river where Pharaoh's daughter used to take a bath. Pharaoh's daughter found him and felt sorry for him and took him in. A Hebrew woman was asked to nurse him and bring him to the palace when he was weaned. So began Moses' journey to the palace of Egypt as he prepared to get on his divine journey.

Moses lived happily in Pharaoh's palace until he was 40 years old. He enjoyed the privileges of a son of Egypt, though he knew he was the biological son of a Hebrew woman. One day he went out to see how his people were doing and saw an Egyptian beating an Israeli slave. After looking round to make sure no one was looking he hit and killed the Egyptian and buried him in the sand, hoping that would end the matter. Eventually the matter did get out and Moses had to flee from Egypt to the wilderness of Midian because even Pharaoh heard about it and sent men to kill him. He fled to the land of Median where he became a shepherd. He met the Jethro family and married his wife Zipporah. He lived in the Land of Median for another forty years until he had an unusual encounter as he tended sheep.

Moses had gone up to Mount Horeb to find pasture for his sheep when he saw a bush on fire and decided to move closer to examine it. On close look, he realised that though the fire was burning, the grass was not being consumed by the flames. That is when he heard a voice speak to him.

> *"And the LORD said, I have surely seen the affliction of my people which are in Egypt, and have heard their cry by reason of their taskmasters; for I know their sorrows; And I am come down to deliver them out of the hand of the Egyptians, and to bring them up out of that land unto a good land and a large, unto a land flowing with milk and honey; unto the place of the Canaanites, and the Hittites, and the Amorites, and the Perizzites, and the Hivites, and the Jebusites. Now therefore, behold, the cry of the children of Israel is come unto me: and I have also seen the oppression wherewith the Egyptians oppress them. Come now therefore, and I will send thee unto Pharaoh, that thou mayest bring forth my people the children of Israel out of Egypt". Exodus 3:7-10.*

The first thing Moses saw was a fire, then an angel of the Lord and then he heard a clear voice instructing him about his mission. He was to go to Pharaoh and demand that he let the Israelites go. Moses' life purpose and mandate was to secure the release of the Israelites from slavery in Egypt. Moses was then 80 years old when he received this clear mandate but as we see all his life was a preparation to carry out this mission. He found favour in the eyes of Pharaoh's daughter at a time when male children were being mercilessly killed. Growing up in the palace meant that when it was time to bargain for the release of his people, he had access to the palace, a privilege which no ordinary Hebrew slave could otherwise have had.

The Dreamer's Experience: Joseph Carpenter, Joseph and Brothers

The use of dreams is another popular way through which people have had things revealed to them with instructions regarding an assignment.

When we go back to the annunciation of the birth of Jesus, we realise that many people were involved and each of the players were contacted in a specific way. Mary received an angelic visitation through a broad daylight vision but Joseph whom she was engaged to be married to, had a dream.

> "Now the birth of Jesus Christ was on this wise: When as his mother Mary was espoused to Joseph, before they came together, she was found with child of the Holy Ghost. Then Joseph her husband, being a just man, and not willing to make her a public example, was minded to put her away privily. But while he thought on these things, behold, the angel of the LORD appeared unto him in a dream, saying, "Joseph, thou son of David, fear not to take unto thee Mary thy wife: for that which is conceived in her is of the Holy Ghost". (Mathew 1:18-20).

This is what I call divine coordination. God was mindful of the fact that Mary was engaged to Joseph and for the divine will to come to pass, Joseph had to be brought into the picture. Imagine the disaster that would have ensued if Joseph had rejected Mary because she was pregnant out of wedlock. The shame, the humiliation and maybe even public stoning of Mary as was the Jewish custom on punishment for such acts of shame. Mary and Jesus needed a safe home to grow in and be nurtured in an atmosphere of stability and normality.

Similarly, in Mathew chapter two after the visit of the wise men, an angel of the Lord appeared to Joseph and instructed him to take Mary and baby Jesus and flee to Egypt because Pharaoh would come looking for the child to kill Him for fear that he would indeed grow up to be king of the Jews and threaten his own kingdom.

Joseph's purpose on earth was to be a husband to Mary, an earthly father to the Messiah. His divine purpose was to raise him, guide him and protect him till he reached the age to fulfil the purpose for which he came to earth. His purpose, as well as the instructions on how to carry it out, was revealed to Joseph principally through dreams. Jacob had four dreams with specific instructions; the first dream advised him to take Mary as wife, the second dream warned him to flee with his family to Egypt, the third dream informed him that Herod and died and he could now return home. On approaching home, Joseph was afraid that Archelaus, Herod's son, was reigning in Judea. So, in yet another dream, an angel of the Lord warned Joseph to take his family to Galilee instead. And it was on the shores of the sea of Galilee that Jesus recruited his first disciples.

Joseph the Dreamer

Another biblical figure famous for his dreams as well as interpretations of dreams was Joseph the son of Jacob. Jacob was born to a large family of boys and because he was born when his father was already an old man, his father loved him very much. As we can imagine when the older boys were out in the fields, the great amount of time these two spent together produced a strong bond between father and son which the other children resented. Jacob's father made it even worse by making Joseph a special coat of many colours to show his love for the lad. This made the older sons hate Jacob the more as this showed clear signs of favouritism on their father's part.

One-night Joseph had a dream. He dreamt that he was in the fields with his brothers and they were all binding sheaves, when his brothers' sheaves rose and bowed down to his sheaf. Joseph was all excited about this dream and foolishly narrated it to his brothers the next day at lunch time thinking they would find it funny. But after recounting his dream to his brothers the angry looks on their faces told him he had made a *faux pas*.

We need to understand how inheritance was passed on from generation to generation to better appreciate this scenario. In most cultures, the father's possessions are the birth right of the first-born son but there have been cases when the father decides for various reasons to hand down his possessions to one other than the first-born son. The boys were furious and asked Joseph if his dreams meant that he will one day rule over them. From the way things were already going their father Jacob already loved him so much and they feared that the dream was an indication of their future.

Joseph dreamt yet another dream that one night, the sun, the moon and stars all bowed to him. Telling his brothers these dreams, amongst others, only helped to fuel their rage against him. It would seem a pattern was forming in which all things were bowing to him and this was worrying. They were so exasperated by his constant dreams that they named him "Joseph the Dreamer". They originally connived to kill him but his elder brother Reuben, the only one who liked him, said they should not spill their brothers blood but throw him into a pit instead. His intention was to come back at night and free his brother. The brothers changed their mind after Reuben left and decided to sell him as a slave to slave merchants. Then they brought his blood-stained coat to their father making him believe a wild beast had eaten his son.

We follow Joseph from the pit to the slave markets in Egypt then to Potiphar's house, where he was thrown into prison and finally became second in command to Pharaoh. While in prison, he interpreted dreams for his inmates and when Pharaoh had a dream that no one could interpret, one of his men remembered Joseph had interpreted his dream before. Joseph was brought before Pharaoh and his interpretation of Pharaoh's dream earned him the position that would today be considered Prime Minister and second in Command.

Now is the time when the purpose for which Joseph was born, the purpose for which he started having all those dreams and the purpose for which he had to go through all the suffering, will begin to make any sense at. Joseph was born to be a counsellor and a deliverer. Through the interpretation of Pharaohs dream, he was able to save Egypt from severe famine, store up food reserves that saved not only Egypt, but the neighbouring countries and his very own brothers who sold him into slavery. God purposed to use Joseph to preserve lives during the famine. True to Joseph's dreams, many people did come and bow to him, including Egyptians. Even his brothers, when they famine hit Israel, hearing there was food in Egypt, went to buy food and did indeed bow to Joseph as his dreams had foretold.

It is important here to note that Joseph's Divine purpose was not for people to bow down to him but for him to help preserve lives in time of severe famine. People bowing to him, was only a by-product of the office he held during the execution of this divine assignment.

Finding Purpose Through Deliberate Creation

In the preceding paragraphs, we see how God can command and manoeuvre people into their divine purpose. In this section, we will see how one can discover their divine purpose through a deliberate creation process.

It would be wrong to suggest that divine intervention in the process of establishing purpose is a thing of the past. God is the

Master of the universe and does everything according to His choosing. Today we have people that are born kings and queens and hold sway over nations. Heirs to the British throne and other monarchies around the world are crowned king as soon as the incumbent steps aside. It does not matter if they are still babies in s a crib. Destiny is thrust upon them. We have children who become movie actors. Michael Jackson, one of the world's most prominent musicians, became a stay at age seven.

Most of the time, however, we have to figure out our divine purpose though a carefully planned process that may involve a lot of steps.

Introducing the S.H.A.P.E Concept

In his book S.H.A.P.E, Erik Rees outlines five pillars on which to build one's quest for their divine purpose.

Now over many years this concept has been tried out in their local church and beyond. Although all human beings are biologically of the same composition, each person, unlike a product on an assembly line, is a unique product. Even identical twins born on the same day have distinguishing characteristics that make them special and exclusive.

SHAPE is a simple acronym which can help people remember 5 factors that God uses to prepare and equip us for our divine purpose: Spiritual gifts, Heart, Abilities, Personality and Experiences.

Let us take a look at these in turn.

Discovering Your Spiritual Gifts

Spiritual gifts can be defined as a set of special abilities given by God to a believer to help him in his Christian journey of loving God and serving the body of believers.

But the manifestation of the Spirit is given to every man to profit withal. For to one is given by the Spirit the word of wisdom; to another the word of knowledge by the same Spirit; To another faith by the same Spirit; to another the gifts of healing by the same Spirit;

To another the working of miracles; to another prophecy; to another discerning of spirits; to another divers kinds of tongues; to another the interpretation of tongues: But all these worketh that one and the selfsame Spirit, dividing to every man severally as he will. For as the body is one, and hath many members, and all the members of that one body, being many, are one body: so also, is Christ. For by one Spirit are we all baptized into one body, whether we be Jews or Gentiles, whether we be bond or free; and have been all made to drink into one Spirit. (1 Corinthians 12: 7-13).

Having then gifts differing according to the grace that is given to us, whether prophecy, let us prophesy according to the proportion of faith; Or ministry, let us wait on our ministering: or he that teaches, on teaching; Or he that exhorteth, on exhortation: he that giveth, let him do it with simplicity; he that rules, with diligence; he that sheweth mercy, with cheerfulness. (Romans 12: 6-8).

As we have seen from the above bible passages the spirit of God is one but individual giftings are varied. Here is a list of spiritual gifts which can be gleaned from this passage

- Word of wisdom
- Word of Knowledge
- Faith,
- Gift of Healing,
- Working of Miracles,
- Gift of Prophecy,
- Discerning of spirits,
- Kinds of Tongues
- Interpretation of Tongues,

- Ministry (Service)
- Teaching
- Exhortation (Encouragement)
- Giving

We can liken this to a tree that has many different parts functioning in different ways. So too is the body of Christ: we have different spiritual gifts which help us function in different offices to fulfil our individual calling and yet compliment the work of the whole body of believers. Knowing what spiritual gifts, a believer has and operates in is a vital tool to fulfilling their divine purpose.

There are also many things we have to guard against. Let's us all remember that God does not give us gifts because we deserve them, because of our looks, or our educational standing, or our aristocratic background. It is a gift and is given to us like grace. It is unmerited favour! The only purpose of our spiritual gifts is to help us in our service and not for ostentation. We need to be wary of spiritual pride as many have let their gifting get to their head.

Some gifts may be more flamboyant such as the gifts of healing, evangelism or administration as opposed to gifts such as mercy and hospitality. Some gifts automatically propel people into the limelight while other gifts may tend to keep people in the background. The essential thing is that we are all part of a team with different roles.

A word of wisdom to leaders as well. Some leaders have the habit of giving awards to people for service and often it seems like people with forefront giftings seem to be the ones recognised more often as their service is usually too glaring to go unnoticed. People with less glowing giftings and forms of service can feel inferior when their service is not recognised. This can create resentment or unhealthy competition. It can also lead to people abandoning what they are called to do in search for offices with greater recognition.

Knowing Your Heart's Desire

Apart from knowing our spiritual gifts another helpful way is to know and understand our hearts desires. The heart is the most important organ of the body as it helps pump blood to all parts of the human system. In the spiritual gifts test, the heart refers to the special passions that God has given an individual. For instance, you have people who grow up and for obvious and sometimes not very obvious reasons, have a passion for children. You see them around children and they feel at home. They desire to love children, play with them, protect them and instruct them. That is their heart's desire and nothing can dissuade them from that.

What is that thing that gives you sleepless lights, or that gets your heart beating faster, that calls you to action with or without reward? As the youth would say what "clicks your switch on". Are you the kind that watches teary eyed a UNESCO broadcast on BBC and want to do everything in your power to help those kids on that disaster torn area?

Are you a childless woman who yearns to give a safe haven for children to grow up in?

Our dear friend Yvonne was adopted at birth by her parents. She never got to know or ever meet her biological parents but the love and care which she received from her parents convinced her that there was no greater love she could have ever received from any other person. She grew up with the philosophy that there are so many children out there who could be given a better life if more families chose adoption or fostering instead of the expensive treatments some undergo for sometimes futile fertility treatments.

Yvonne and her husband Tom have adopted 3 children and fostered 7 more children single handed. Although she has no medical condition that prevents her from having children of her own, Yvonne and her husband Tom, have deprived themselves of the privilege of child birth to pour their love into other children. The love her adoptive parents planted in her left a mark so indelible in her soul that all she could dream of was to do the same for others. Her home at Christmas is a sight to behold. Cars upon cars parked in the neighbouring driveways to accommodate all the kids, foster kids and foster grand kids coming home to the place where they were loved and nurtured into life.

Passion is a fascination. It is waking up in the morning and it being one of the first thoughts in your head. Passion is not stopping until you've reached your goal, because you know that if you don't put in the work you won't see the results. Find out the things that you care deeply about.

One such person who followed her heart's desire is Mother Theresa of Calcutta whom we shall discuss in another chapter.

Harnessing Your Abilities

Another indicator of one's life purpose can be gleaned by exploring an individual's personal abilities. Every one of us is born with a talent, a gift, an ability through which they express themselves. No single individual has all the talents in the world even though it may seem like that when we watch some people excelling in their gifting. Nobody has it all but we all have something. That is why the apostle Paul, exhorts Christians in the book of Romans chapter 12 on how to each handle their respective spiritual gifts. No one should think of themselves or their gifts as higher or better than others but each should concentrate in serving with their individual gifts in order to contribute to the wholeness of the body of Christ. I personally think that one's natural talents should be given a lot of consideration when trying to understand divine purpose.

Let us take the music ministry for example. Before you think of joining the choir, there must be some innate quality in your voice for singing. I know there are award winning music teachers that can work miracles with amazing coaching but those are exceptions. I know as a pastor with several years of experience in the ministry that many of these Christians do it out of a pure desire to serve God in whatever way is available. But if you can't sing, you can't play an instrument and are not able to learn, then serving in this area will be a long stretch.

The key words here are observation and exploration. From the time a child is born the parents begin to observe the things the child is good at or seems to show a penchant for. The next thing you see parents doing is trying to buy toys that will help these kids explore the talents which they seem to have observed. Every parents joy and nightmare is the warehouse of abandoned toys and gadgets amassing dust in their basements. But as much as they may complain about it, it is every parent's wish to do everything they can to help their offspring develop their talents.

Soul searching and self-discovery are advised. Ask yourself what gifts and talents you have. If it is not as obvious as is the case with many gifts, find out what you are good at naturally? Some people are gifted orators. They can talk for hours and you could listen to them without getting bored. We once held a couples' convention in our church with a family weekend and parents were allowed to bring their kids. After the day's activities, the kids were so hyper none of them wanted to sleep. Parent after parent went in and told them off just for the noise to resume as soon as the door was shut. We were exasperated and all we wanted was to sleep. Then we realised that there was a sudden unexpected, almost eerie silence. One of the mums went to check the kids to be sure they were okay. One of the older girls, Patricia, had made them all sit in a circle and she was reading a bedtime story to them. Some had already fallen asleep on the floor while the rest of the kids listened to their mate with rapt attention. Needless to say, Patricia later on took on a career in early years education and excelled in it. It has been a pleasure to watch her unfold as a young teacher offering her services both to the secular world as a devoted nursery teacher as well as helping the church design and run kids' programmes.

Leveraging Your Personality

The Oxford dictionary describes personality as the unique set of traits and qualities that make up a person's character.

Imagine someone with a shy personality wanting to become a motivational speaker when they can't even speak up for someone to decipher what they are saying. Becoming a motivational speaker requires an outgoing and bold personality. It takes a person who is fearless, erudite and convincing to become one. Some people are so scared of crowds that even a simple shopping trip to a mall or supermarket looks like a ride to hell. Are you the person who is always sitting in a corner by themselves at every social gathering or are you the one whom everyone is always around as you wow them with tale after tale of exploits?

If you observe a classroom it is very easy to spot out kids with outgoing and spontaneous personalities. Now they may not always have the correct answers but they are quick to raise their hands at every question. Sometimes by the time the teacher calls them they have already forgotten what they wanted to say but their hands will be back up at the next opportunity. As you try to figure out what God's purpose for your life is, try to find out how your God-given personality will help you find and fulfil that role.

I must add here that even though some personality traits are inborn and appear to be almost fossilised, in my years of ministry, I have seen and mentored Christians as they arise from a timid personality and blossom into confident outgoing people fulfilling roles, they could never have dreamed they could even venture into. Let us not forget that someone like Moses in the bible was a stutterer, yet it was him that God chose to command and lead the people of Israel out of Egypt.

Drawing From Your Experiences

There is a saying that we all throw around casually ever day: "experience is the best teacher". Nothing could be truer than this statement. The scripture says in Romans 8:28

> *"And we know that all things work together for good to them that love God, to them who are the called according to his purpose."*

As a Christian, this is one of the scriptures I struggled to understand or accept but the sooner we make peace with this scripture the better we will be able to understand the treasure of lessons that accompany our everyday experiences. I realise that it is difficult to accept that God uses all the positive and negative experiences in our lives for good but in life there are many instances of how peoples' life experiences have helped them to be of better service. We live in a culture where success is celebrated and failure is pushed aside and never talked about but I dare us to look back at the instances in our lives when we failed, went through pain and disappointment and walked through it to emerge even stronger on the other side.

It is my hope that this chapter has shed enough light on how we can focus on finding our divine purpose.

Having found our purpose, there are certain ingredients we need to strengthen it and put it into action.

That would be the focus of Chapter 6.

CHAPTER 6

VITAL KEYS TO MANIFESTING YOUR PURPOSE

"Once you have defined your aims and what you want, it is easier to deal with doubts". Viktor E. Frankl

IN CHAPTER 5 we saw how divine purpose can be revealed by a more dramatic intervention by God and through the subtler method of deliberate creation.

In this very important chapter, we will work from the premise that you have already discovered your divine purpose and are ready to put it in action. In order to be able to do that effectively, we will discuss certain keys or tools you would need to fulfil your divine purpose with confidence.

Prayer and Divine Purpose

We all know that prayer is the centre of all we do and that without it we are powerless. Prayer is a relationship, wherein we humbly communicate, worship, and sincerely seek God's face, knowing that He hears us, loves us and will respond, though not always in a manner we may expect or desire. Prayer can encompass confession, praise, adoration, supplication, intercession and more.

In addition, our attitude in prayer is important. We must not be haughty, but humble (Ephesians 4:2; James 4:10; 1 Peter 5:6, etc.). Seen in this light, to "pray continually" (1 Thessalonians 5:17) means, in one sense, that we must always strive to have a prayerful attitude. Our prayers must come often and regularly, not from legalistic duty, but from a humble heart, realizing our dependence on God in every aspect of our lives.

The most important reason why we need to pray for our divine purpose to be fulfilled is that **prayer gives us direction** in everything we do:

> "Trust in the Lord with all thine heart; and lean not unto thine own understanding. In all thy ways acknowledge him, and he shall direct thy paths". (Proverbs 3: 5-7).

Another reason why we must pray often is that **prayer gives us strength**. 2 Corinthians 12: 9 says:

> "And he said unto me, My grace is sufficient for thee: for my strength is made perfect in weakness. Most gladly therefore will I rather glory in my infirmities, that the power of Christ may rest upon me".

Prayer also takes away anxiety regarding your divine purpose.

God's word reassures us that when doubts and tough times arise, we do not have to fear:

> "Fear thou not; for I am with thee: be not dismayed; for I am thy God: I will strengthen thee; yea, I will help thee; yea, I will uphold thee with the right hand of my righteousness."

In Philippians 4:6–8 His word encourages us to:

> "Be careful for nothing; but in everything by prayer and supplication with thanksgiving let your requests be made known unto God. And the peace of God, which passes all understanding, shall keep your hearts and minds through Christ Jesus".

Prayer also **keeps God near to us as a companion** as we carry out our divine purpose. *"And behold, I am with you always, to the end of the age". (Matthew 28:20).*

It is clear from the above that we have all we need through prayer to fulfil our divine purpose. I love the song that says:

> *Great is Thy faithfulness, O God my Father;*
> *There is no shadow of turning with Thee;*
> *Thou changest not, Thy compassions, they fail not;*
> *As Thou hast been, Thou forever wilt be.*
> *Summer and winter and springtime and harvest,*
> *Sun, moon and stars in their courses above*
> *Join with all nature in manifold witness*
> *To Thy great faithfulness, mercy and love.*

> *Great is Thy faithfulness!*
> *Great is Thy faithfulness!*
> *Morning by morning new mercies I see.*
> *All I have needed Thy hand hath provided;*
> *Great is Thy faithfulness, Lord, unto me!*

> *Pardon for sin and a peace that endures*
> *Thine own dear presence to cheer and to guide;*
> *Strength for today and bright hope for tomorrow,*
> *Blessings all mine, with ten thousand beside!*

Arise son or daughter of Almighty God and fulfil your divine purpose. Resting in the confidence that He directs you, strengthens you, reassures you and stands with you at all time. We say also in Chapter 4 that through His redemption, "all [you] hath needed His Hands hath provided".

As you set out every day to carry out your divine purpose, please say this prayer before you step out. You can rephrase it to suit your purpose.

Thank You Father that I am Your child and that I have a citizenship laid up for me in the heaven, from which we await our coming Saviour, the Lord Jesus Christ. Thank You that Your purpose for humanity is all tied up in Him, and that He is to be honoured above all rule and authority... power and dominion, and every name that is named, not only in this age but also in the one to come.

Thank You Father that You have put all things in subjection under His feet, and given Him as Head over all things to the Church, which is His body - the fullness of Him Who fills all in all. Heavenly Father, as a part of that Body I pray that I may fulfil the divine duty that You have purposed for me to do. I thank You Father that Your will for my life is to transform me into the image and likeness of the Lord Jesus Christ and I pray that my life may reflect His grace and beauty in all I say and do.

I pray that I may willingly submit to the work of the Holy Spirit in my life — even on those occasions when I do not understand... and ask that all that is of me may decrease and all that is of Christ may increase — until He is all in all in my life... to Your praise and glory. This I ask in the name of Jesus. Amen.

Faith and Divine Purpose

Carrying out your divine purpose involves faith most of the time. You see, your divine purpose may appear to you and seem scary. Remember Moses? The mission to "set my people free" was so daunting that he tried to bargain his way out of it. It took faith to see through the mission. Consider Joseph of the Old Testament. He is an example of someone who could have been deceived by focusing on what met the eye. The pit his brothers threw him into after he revealed his prophetic dreams to them looked like the end of his dreams! (See Gen. 37.) Joseph could have considered himself defeated, but he kept the faith.

In Potiphar's house, when things turned from bad to worse for him, Joseph continued to trust God—who took the pit and made it the very vehicle that moved Joseph in the direction of the palace, the fulfilment of his dreams (see Gen. 39-41).

Now think about your own life. Regardless of the way things look, God has a wonderful purpose for you. You may be stuck in a dead-end job and struggling to pay your bills. You may be suffering from a debilitating illness and wondering if you can cope with that task ahead. I love the song *"That's When He Steps In"* by Alvin Slaughter that goes:

> *"When we have a work to do*
> *And the task ahead seems bigger than you*
> *That's when He steps in*
> *When you know in your heart that God's command*
> *Takes more than can be done by man*
> *That's when He steps in*
> *He sees you at the point of your need*
> *He sees you at the point of crossing your Red Sea*

Hebrews 11 gets me every time I feel I cannot fulfil my divine purpose. I dare you to read the whole book and not be fired up to press on with the vision. After highlighting the faith of Abraham, Noah, Abel, Enoch, Isaac and a host of others, the writer goes on to say from verses 32-40:

> *"And what shall I more say? for the time would fail me to tell of Gedeon, and of Barak, and of Samson, and of Jephthah; of David also, and Samuel, and of the prophets: Who through faith subdued kingdoms, wrought righteousness, obtained promises, stopped the mouths of lions, Quenched the violence of fire, escaped the edge of the sword, out of weakness were made strong, waxed valiant in fight, turned to flight the armies of the aliens. Women received their dead raised to life again: and others were tortured, not accepting deliverance; that they might obtain a better resurrection: And others had trial of cruel mockings and scourgings, yea, moreover*

of bonds and imprisonment: They were stoned, they were sawn asunder, were tempted, were slain with the sword: they wandered about in sheepskins and goatskins; being destitute, afflicted, tormented; (Of whom the world was not worthy:) they wandered in deserts, and in mountains, and in dens and caves of the earth. And these all, having obtained a good report through faith, received not the promise: God having provided some better thing for us, that they without us should not be made perfect".

Where is the evidence? Since God is Spirit (see John 4:24), He often moves in ways we can't see. That's why we need faith—defined in Hebrews 11:1 as, "the substance of things hoped for, the evidence of things not seen." We get glimpses of God and the evidence of His work through our faith.

Today, as you ponder the great miracles wrought by these servants of God, I challenge you to join me in dwelling not on the evidence of your divine purpose, but on the God of your calling—the God who is faithful (see 1 Thess. 5:24), the God who will make it happen, just as His Word promises (see Phil. 1:6), the same God who brought Joseph from the pit to the palace.

The God of your calling cares about what you see. He also cares about what you don't always see—the evidence of things yet to come.

Arise and shine!

Education, Training and Divine Purpose

Carrying out your divine purpose involves a particular set of skills which you may already have or may need to develop. Even the most obvious of tasks may require some form of education and training. If your divine purpose is revealed as a pilot whose role it is to transport men of God over long distances using aircraft, you would need to take lessons in aviation and perhaps obtain your Private Pilot's Licence (PPL). If you are called upon to be an architect to build churches, you may have to acquire architectural skills if you do not already have them.

When we come into this world, we are tabular rasa and we need to work on ourselves to be able to carry out the task that is laid before us. 2 Timothy 2:15 says:

> *"Study to shew thyself approved unto God, a workman that needeth not to be ashamed, rightly dividing the word of truth".*

The Lord Himself knows that we need to acquire knowledge. I am horrified each time I ponder the skewed "wisdom" of those that suggest that prayer can take the place of study. It can't. Education gives us the ability to analyse and troubleshoot. It enables us to overcome challenges. It also allows us to have a clearer vision of things. In order to fully carry out your divine vision, you may require an education and training to prepare you.

A word of caution. God may freely use anyone, even those without a formal education, to fulfil his purpose. We all know about Smith Wigglesworth and his extraordinary ministry. Often referred to as 'the Apostle of Faith,' Wigglesworth was one of the pioneers of the Pentecostal revival that occurred a century ago. Without human refinement and education, he was able to tap into the infinite resources of God to bring divine grace to multitudes.

Thousands came to Christian faith in his meetings, hundreds were healed of serious illnesses and diseases as supernatural signs followed his ministry. A deep intimacy with his heavenly Father and an unquestioning faith in God's Word brought spectacular results and provided an example for all true believers of the Gospel.

As you read this book, you may feel a stirring in your heart to go out and do something the Lord has always asked you to do. Do not let your lack of education hold you back. Go forth in faith and allow the Spirit of the Living God to take control.

Goal Setting and Divine Purpose

Your divine vision is a very serious matter. It is an instruction from God to go out and do something. That's how serious it is. Thankfully, when God says to go and do something, He has your back.

The next step after determining your divine purpose is to develop your personal vision – a clear idea of where you want to be in a few months or years, and why. This is a crucial part of developing your purpose. Say God has given you a purpose to provide homes for homeless people. This is a huge undertaking which involves elaborate planning. You must first of all map out the vision and all that it involves. Luke 14:28 says, *"For which of you, intending to build a tower, sitteth not down first, and counteth the cost, whether he have sufficient to finish it"?*

Goal setting will help you in fulfilling your divine purpose in a number of ways:

1. Goals Give You Focus

Imagine having to shoot an arrow without being given a target. Where would you aim? And say you did aim at some random thing (out of sheer perplexity). Why would you aim there? And what would the purpose be? Get the idea? This is a literal example of what life is like without a goal or target in mind. It's pointless and a waste of energy and effort. You can have all the potential in the world but without focus your abilities and talent are useless. Just like how sunlight can't burn through anything without a magnifying glass focusing it, you can't achieve anything unless a goal is focusing your effort. Because at the end of the day goals are what give you direction in life. By setting goals for yourself you give yourself a target to shoot for. This sense of direction is what allows your mind to focus on a target and rather than waste energy shooting aimlessly, allows you to hit your target and reach your goal. Zig Ziglar says "If you aim at nothing, you will hit it every time".

2. Goals Allow You To Measure Progress

By setting goals for your divine purpose you are able to measure your progress because you always have a fixed endpoint or benchmark to compare with. Take this scenario for example: David makes a goal to write a book with a minimum of 300 pages. He starts writing every day and works really hard but along the way, he loses track of how many more pages he has written and how much more he needs to write. So rather than panicking David simply counts the number of pages he has already written and he instantly determines his progress and knows how much further he needs to go.

3. Goals Keep You Locked in And Undistracted

By setting goals for your divine purpose, you give yourself mental boundaries. When you have a certain end point in mind you automatically stay away from certain distractions and stay focused towards the goal. This process happens automatically and subtly but according to research does happen. To get a better idea, imagine this. Your best friend is moving to Switzerland and his flight takes off at 9:00 PM. You leave right after work at 8:30 PM to see him off and you know it's a 20-minute walk to get to the airport. So, you make it a goal to reach the airport in 15 minutes by jogging so that you can have more time to say your goodbyes. Would you get distracted by "anything" along the way? Would you stop for a break or a snack? Would you stop by your house before going to the airport? I bet you answered no for each question and at the end of the day, this is what a goal gives you. FOCUS. No matter who you meet along the way or what you see (assuming nothing is out of the ordinary) your goal allows you to stay locked in. You subconsciously keep away from distractions and your focus remains only on the goal. And by the way if you didn't know yet this is how you become successful, you set a goal, you lock it in and then give it your 100%. Sidney Howard says "one half of knowing what you want, is knowing what you must give up before you get it".

4. Goals Help You Overcome Procrastination

When you set a goal for yourself you make yourself accountable to finish the task. This is in complete contrast with when you do things based off a whim and it doesn't matter whether you complete them or not. Goals tend to stick in your mind and if not completed they give you a "Shoot! I was supposed to do _____ today!" reminder. These reminders in the back of your head help you to overcome procrastination and laziness. (*But keep in mind that long-term goals actually promote procrastination. Most people aren't good with deadliness 3 months away. So, whenever you're given a long-term goal, break it down into several short-term goals so you can complete a chunk of the larger long-term goal every week or even every day.)

5. Goals Give You Motivation

The root of all the motivation or inspiration you have ever felt in your entire life are goals. Goal setting provides you the foundation for your drive. By making a goal you give yourself a concrete endpoint to aim for and get excited about. It gives you something to focus on and put 100% of your effort into and this focus is what develops motivation. Goals are simply tools to focus your energy in positive directions, these can be changed as your priorities change, new ones added, and others dropped.

So, if you want to achieve all the plans that are associated with your divine purpose, it is important that you set clear goals and work toward achieving them.

Self-Image and Divine Purpose

We saw in Chapter 3 how a low self-esteem can torpedo your divine purpose. Most of us are better, wiser, stronger and more competent right now than we realize. There is a clear correlation between our image of ourselves and what we become, achieve or obtain in life.

In his ground-breaking book The New Psycho-Cybernetics, Dr Maxwell Maltz puts forward some of the best arguments regarding the connection between self-image and achievement or failure:

> *"Whether we realize it or not, each of us carries within us a mental blueprint or picture of ourselves. It may be vague and ill-defined to our conscious gaze. In fact, it may not be consciously recognizable at all. But it is there, complete down to the last detail. This self-image is our own conception of the 'sort of person I am'. It has been built up from our own beliefs about ourselves. Most of these beliefs about ourselves have been unconsciously formed from our past experiences, our successes and failures, our humiliations, our triumphs, and the way other people have reacted to us, especially in early childhood.*
>
> *From all these we mentally construct a self (or a picture of a self). Once an idea or a belief about ourselves goes into this picture, it becomes 'truth', as far as we personally are concerned. We do not question its validity, but proceed to act upon it just as if it were true.*
>
> *The self-image then controls what you can and cannot accomplish, what is difficult or easy for you, even how others respond to you just as certainly and scientifically as a thermostat controls the temperature in your home. Specifically, all your actions, feelings, behaviour, even your abilities, are always consistent with this self-image. Note the word: always. In short, you will 'act like' the sort of person you conceive yourself to be. More important, you literally cannot act otherwise, in spite of all your conscious efforts or willpower. (This is why trying to achieve something difficult with teeth gritted is a losing battle. Willpower is not the answer. Self-image management is)".*

When this self-image is set, you cannot outperform it. If you perform above it, you will be "snapped back" to your usual level. Self-image in the Bible is encapsulated by the simple, yet powerful verse in Proverbs 23:7 which says that *"as a man thinketh in his heart, so is he"*. Self-image is centrifugal to the life of any Christian who aspires to carry out their divine purpose. This is even the more so because the church has been for far too long the most significant influence on the life of the Christian. Christians need to arise and shine. They need to take up their position with the King. They need to be the princes that ride on horseback, not those that walk on foot!

There is therefore the urgent need to "be transformed by the renewing of your mind". (Romans 12: 2). The Bible assures us in Genesis 1:26 that we were created in the image and likeness of God. We all know that God is perfect, infallible and a success in everything. So are you. You were "fearfully and wonderfully made", appointed as a "joint heir" to the throne and given dominion over everything in the earth. You are a walking wonder. Think about it. You can demand instant audience with the Master of the Universe and you do not need an appointment. Hebrews 4:16 says:

> *"Let us therefore come boldly to the throne of grace, that we may obtain mercy, and find grace to help in time of need".*

That is why it beats me that some Christians abandon their divine purpose and the first sound of gunfire. Years of prayer and fasting could not have gone in vain. Somehow, a lot of us know what our divine purpose is. We are just not confident enough to take them on!

Our churches are awash with Generals working as bus drivers, bestselling authors working as factory hands, CEOs working as cleaners, senior level managers working as secretaries, bankers serving as barmaids. No more! Enough is enough! Look at yourself in the mirror right now and shout ENOUGH IS ENOUGH!

Self-image deficiency can, thankfully, be corrected. Look at all those around you who are accomplishing great things with ease. Look at them carefully. A lot of them do not have any better skills than yourself. They are not more intelligent than yourself. They just believe in themselves.

Does your divine vision look too daunting for you? Then turn on the stereo and sing the song by Bob Fitts that says:

> *I know I can do all things*
> *I can do all things through Christ*
> *With the power of God and the Word of Life*
> *I can do all things (I can do all things)*
> *I can do all things through Christ*
>
> *God is the One who strengthens me*
> *With faith to overcome*
> *Now I can be sure of the victory*

Once you have dealt with your self-image, programmed yourself for success, looked in the mirror and seen that you are ready, the world is now at your feet and you can now set your goal, any goal, and be sure of its achievement. Deuteronomy 28:13 says:

> *"...The Lord shall make thee the head, and not the tail; and thou shalt be above only, and thou shalt not be beneath".*

Get up right this minute and grab that divine purpose by the scruff of the neck and show the world that *"Some things may be impossible with men; but with God all things are possible"! (Mark 10:27).*

PART 3

HOW TO FULFIL YOUR DIVINE PURPOSE

CHAPTER 7

THE SEED PRINCIPLE
OF ALL CREATION

"Anyone can count the seeds in an apple, but only God can count the number of apples in a seed" – Robert H. Schuller

YOUR DREAMS; YOUR thoughts; your words; your deeds or actions, even your 'givings' including your prayers are all seeds of creation!

You are in charge of your destiny by the seeds of creation you are (sowing) releasing. Every seed produces after its own kind – Genesis 1:12

To conceive and give birth to anything you will ever need in life; You must first and foremost plant God's Word for that need like a seed in your heart (which is the soil of life). Conception can never take place without first planting the seed of life.

A seed is anything you can contribute to another. It is anything you are capable of giving away! An hour of your time invested in someone with a need, is a seed. Kind words, friendship, loyalty, including money – Anything that you plant towards people or God's work is what is call a seed.

Life gives you options; you make your choices by the decisions you take or make moment by moment. Every little, little deeds are like seeds – They grow to flowers or to weeds of life.

Your purpose is the seed of your life. The seed of life is the trigger for all the contentions a man will face in life. This is because everything in life stems from the seed of its purpose.

Your thoughts and dreams (visions) are the seeds of your purpose(s) in life. Nothing in life ever grows without a seed, and nothing ever changes without inspired dream(s) triggered by eternal purpose. The smallest seed of the word sown into a pure and honest heart – Has the capacity to grow into the greatest tree in the world (Mark 4:30-33).

Every man's heart is full of fertile seeds, waiting to sprout. This is the beauty of creation born out of the fairness to all creation by the ever-faithful creator.

It was Joyce Meyer, a well-known International Television Evangelist who said: "God has equipped every man to handle difficult things. Infact, He Has already planted the seeds of discipline and self-control inside you. You just have to water those seeds with His creative words to make them grow."

Whatever seeds each and every man cultivates will grow to maturity and bear in and for him their own fruits. The great and goodness of creation however is that the seeds of passion are innate to all mankind, and nobody comes into this world without them.

God's Word is alive and powerful! When a man consistently declares these words over his life, the truth and the Spirit of God's Words draw and bring forth the seeds of God's nature in him into manifestation.

In the same vein, your own words are also your personal seeds. When your words are released into the invisible spiritual substance (as you speak and pray), they grow and bring forth after their kind – "Every plant produces its own kind of seed."

Fruits are always the same nature with the seeds and roots from which they originate; Trees are also known by the fruits they bear – As a man begets a man. Norman Vincent Peale posited that: "Every problem has in it the seeds of its own solution." He further stated: "If you don't have any problems, you don't get any seeds."

"You were designed for accomplishment, engineered for success, and endowed with the seeds of greatness" – Zig Ziglar.

The Word of God often refers to itself as a seed – Saint Luke's Gospel Chapter 8 Verse Number 11. To bring about the manifestation of your purpose in life, you must first plant God's Word for your purpose like a seed in your heart. Conception can never ever take place in natural reproduction (human creation) without first planting the seed of it. There has only been one virgin birth in the entire universe. The birth, release and manifestation of your own purpose on earth will never be the second one.

In the Gospel according to Saint Mark Chapter Number 4, the Lord Jesus Christ taught three parables which illustrate that the Word is to the Kingdom of God what a natural seed is to a harvest. The first of these parables, the story of the sower, is the key to unlocking all the word of God – Mark 4:13 If this fundamental principle of creation is not understood – The Greatest Teacher of all times said; No man can understand any of His other parables or principles.

Never judge each day by the harvest you reap but by the seeds that you plant. It is only the farmer who faithfully plants seeds in the Spring, who reaps a harvest in the Autumn. Anyone can count the seeds in an apple, but only the Lord can count the number of apples in a seed.

A man can cheat or manipulate nearly all systems that men have created. The Legal or Justice System can be beaten, letting the guilty go free. The Education System can be cornered, passing students who have not really learned the materials. But no man can short-circuit or change the seedtime and harvest principle of creation.

The Scripture (God's Word) is a spiritual seed – Luke 8:11. It never expires. It lingers through all generations – forever! 1 Peter 1:23. The seed of the word received empowers to become! (John 1:12)

Imagine if a farmer waited until he saw his neighbours reaping their crops before he sowed for his own crops! Regardless of how sincere he may be, or his justification for not sowing his seed at the appropriate time – He would not reap any crop overnight. The law of seedtime and harvest cannot be violated or manipulated.

The law of seedtime and harvest operates in every area of our lives. If we will plant God's Words in our hearts, then allow the seed to germinate and the plant to grow to maturity, we will reap the fruits of bountiful harvests.

Dreams are the seeds of change. Nothing ever grows in life without a seed, and nothing ever changes in life without a dream. Little deeds are like little seeds, they grow to flowers or to weeds.

You reap what you sow. What you work for is what you will get. Do not expect to get success if you do not do what needs to be done. Everything you do, everything you say, every choice you make, sooner or later comes back around.

If you want change, then make the change. If you want to be treated well, then treat others well. If you want to be loved, then love others. Do not expect to get something when you are not doing it yourself. Too many people expect perfection from others yet fail to give out what they expect.

It was Charles Reade who said: "Sow a thought, and you reap an act; Sow an act, and you reap a habit; Sow a habit and you reap a character; Sow a character, and you reap a destiny." You reap what you sow in life. "Those who brings sunshine to the lives of others cannot keep it from themselves." (J.M. Barrie).

Like a boomerang – our thoughts, deeds and words return to us sooner or later, with astounding accuracy. Life is like a garden; you reap what you sow.

You reap in Sales, what you sow in Marketing. God wants to use you to make other people happy. The happier you make others, the happier you will be because, you reap what you sow. You will never change your life until you change your choices. You reap what you sow. You become what you continually think and do.

Be the reflection of what you would like to see in others. If you want love, give love. If you want honesty, give honesty. If you want respect, give respect. You will always get in return whatever you give. What you sow, you reap. It is a law of nature. Your mind is your garden of life; You can grow flowers. You can as well grow weeds. What you sow is what you reap.

CHAPTER 8

THE POWER OF HUMAN IMAGINATION/(THOUGHTS)

"Your imagination is your preview of life's coming attractions." Albert Einstein

YOUR IMAGINATION IS an invisible machine inside your mind. It is given to all "homo-sapiens" – human beings, to create pictures of whatever is their heart desires.

IMAGINATION is the workshop of the human mind wherein old ideas and established facts may be re-assembled into new combinations and put to new uses.

Webster's Third International Dictionary defines imagination as:

1. An act or process of forming a conscious idea or mental image of something never before wholly perceived in reality by the imaginer (as through a synthesis of remembered elements of previous sensory experiences or ideas ….)
2. Creative ability ….; Resourcefulness ….

Just as the oak tree develops from the germ that lies in the acorn, and the bird develops from the germ that lies asleep in the egg, so will your fulfilment of divine purpose grow out of the inspired thoughts and organised plans that you create in your imagination. Primarily, with the thoughts; then organisation of the thoughts into ideas and plans; then transformation of those plans into physical or tangible reality.

Your mind functions through imagination that is, through your thoughts. You cannot do anything without imagination.

You are one decision away from living the life of your dreams and purposes. Your destiny moves at the speed of thoughts. The quality of your life is determined by the quality of your thoughts. You have complete sovereignty over the territory of your mind. You will never become more tomorrow than who you think you are today. (Proverbs 4:23 & 23:7) You will never go where your mind cannot take you. "You can do it if you believe you can!"

One of the meanings of the word "imagination" in the Old Testament is "conception". Your imagination is the mental function or faculty where you can see things – conceive ideas! Without your imagination, you would be totally non-creative and unproductive.

There are basically two ways by which human beings "see" things: Physical Vision through the eyes, or by their Imagination.

Without imagination, mankind would be completely limited and virtually robotic! All human progresses have been born out of imagination – The ability to "SEE" things as they could be or differently than they were.

The only way human beings can see the past or the future un-aided, is through their imagination. Memory uses the imagination. Much of our thinking, whether planning or "jumping to conclusions", involves the use of imagination. Fear and Faith operate in the realm of imagination.

Many top athletes successfully use their imagination in training. Vividly imagining a successful action seems to be more effective in training than doing it physically. When we experience an event vividly in our imagination, it is imprinted as an experience; even though we did not physically do it.

Children seem to naturally have active imaginations. As we grow older and become more "educated", we tend to use our imaginations less. Everyone has used their imagination negatively by worrying. We should use the same process in a positive way, based on the the divine counsel as written in the Epistle to the Philippians in Chapter Number 4; Verse Number 8.

One of the most beautiful and gracious gifts of God in all mankind is the mind. There are two major functions of the mind: Memory and Imagination. The memory photograph, file and replay pictures of your past. While the imagination on the other hand, creates and replays pictures of things you want to happen in your future.

There is a fascinating story in Genesis Chapter Number 11 which illustrates the power of the imagination in practical term. The Babylonians wanted to build a city and tower that would reach into heaven. This was like a contention with the Almighty. Hence, He was displeased and so confused their tongues and scattered them abroad.

However, there is a particularly remarkable observation in the sixth verse about the people and their ability to picture the goals they had set for themselves. "And the Lord said: Behold, the people is one, and they have all one language; and this they begin to do: AND NOW NOTHING WILL BE RESTRAINED FROM THEM, WHICH THEY HAVE IMAGINED TO DO."

Your imagination – Your thought life controls you. Hence, the Scripture admonished that: "…. Whatsoever things are true, whatsoever things are honest, whatsoever things are just, whatsoever things are pure, whatsoever things are lovely, whatsoever things are of good report; if there be any virtue, and if there be any praise, think or meditate on these things" – Philippians 4:8.

According to 2 Corinthians 4:18 (NKJV) – "While we do not look at the things which are seen, but at the things which are not seen. For the things which are seen are temporary, but the things which are not seen are eternal. How can a man look at things which are not seen? This can only be done by the power of human imagination – through thoughts.

To the builder, his blueprint is his conception. First an idea, then a mental picture which he imagines, and then the drawn blueprint. The picture you imagine is the seed of something that will be born later from it. Its imagination is the mental rehearsal before it is acted out and eventually created or produced.

Your imagination is the creative part of you. It is the seed of your actions. Your imagination functions whether you are aware of it or not. In every situation, you are imagining what is going to happen or how it will turn out. You are always picturing in your mind what you are thinking about. Your imagination is a by-product of where your focus is.

You don't get to choose whether you imagine or not. The only thing you get to choose is whether your imagination is working for you or against you. Your image of yourself determines who you are. What you see is what you become – "As a man thinks in his heart, so is he." (Proverbs 23:7a) Worry is a vivid imagination in the negative realm.

> THE FUTURE BELONGS TO THOSE WHO BELIEVE IN THE BEAUTY OF THEIR DREAMS – Eleanor Roosevelt.

> TO KNOW IS NOTHING AT ALL; TO IMAGINE IS EVERYTHING – Anatole France.

> DREAM. DREAM BIG DREAMS! OTHERS MAY DEPRIVE YOU OF YOUR MATERIAL WEALTH AND CHEAT YOU IN A THOUSAND WAYS, BUT NO MAN CAN DEPRIVE YOU OF THE CONTROL AND USE OF YOUR IMAGINATION. MEN MAY DEAL WITH YOU UNFAIRLY, AS MEN OFTEN DO; THEY MAY DEPRIVE YOU OF YOUR LIBERTY; BUT

THEY CANNOT TAKE FROM YOU THE PRIVILEGE OF USING YOUR IMAGINATION. IN YOUR IMAGINATION YOU ALWAYS WIN – Jesse Jackson.

CHAPTER 9

YOUR PURPOSE IS YOUR DIVINE ASSIGNMENT

"The mystery of human existence lies not in just staying alive, but in finding something to live for." Fyodor Dostoyevsky

I CAME ACROSS a quote in the Harvard Business Review which can help start off this chapter. It says, "You must also envision the impact you'll have on your world as a result of living your purpose". Each time I think of divine purpose, I see an orchestra producing beautiful music. The violinist simply follows their own notes and plays. The keyboardist does the same. The drummer simply plays to the song sheet. Most of the time, they do not even look at each other. They simply do what they are meant to be doing. The result is a smooth blend of well-orchestrated notes that produces soothing music.

As it is in the kingdom; So is it in the world we live in. The great Shakespeare once said that "All the world is a stage, and all the men and women merely players". Very apt. We come into the world to play a particular part which when added to the whole, brings harmony to the universe.

The way I see divine purpose, it should accomplish two things. First, it should contribute to mankind's well-being and happiness. Second, it should glorify God and help expand his Kingdom. In a moment, we will be looking at some forebears of divine purpose who, by following their divine purpose, made the world a better place and have since helped to grow the Kingdom of God. First, we will look at biblical examples and they move on to study secular cases.

Biblical Examples of People Who Fulfilled Their Purpose

The bible tells many exciting stories of men and women who walked in their purposes, changed the world and enriched God's government.

Jesus Christ Saviour of All Mankind

Jesus remains the greatest example when it comes to fulfilling divine purpose. It is almost embarrassing that whenever people are asked to give examples of individuals who have found and fulfilled their purpose, Christians begin to scratch their heads and bite their finger nails looking for examples to put forward when their very own saviour stands before them as the most glaring example of a purpose-led life.

Right from the book of Genesis, even without the mention of the name of Christ there is a promise spoken about the coming of Jesus who will be the seed of the woman that will bruise the head of the serpent. Gods purpose for sending Jesus into the world was so that he could suffer and die on the cross for the sole purpose of reconciling mankind back to fellowship with God. This coming of Jesus was foretold throughout the ages by prophets.

Isaiah 7:14 foretold Jesus' birth in these words "Therefore the Lord himself will give you a sign: The virgin will be with child and will give birth to a son, and will call him Immanuel." Isaiah 9:6: "For to us a child is born, to us a son is given, and the government will be on his shoulders. And he will be called Wonderful Counsellor, Mighty God, Everlasting Father, Prince of Peace." Micah 5:2: "But you, Bethlehem Ephrathah, though you are small among the clans of Judah, out of you will come for me one who will be ruler over Israel, whose origins are from of old, from ancient times."

Concerning Jesus' ministry and death, Zechariah 9:9 says, "Rejoice greatly, O Daughter of Zion! Shout, Daughter of Jerusalem! See, your king comes to you, righteous and having salvation, gentle and riding on a donkey, on a colt, the foal of a donkey." Psalm 22:16-18: "Dogs have surrounded me; a band of evil men has encircled me; they have pierced my hands and my feet. I can count all my bones; people stare and gloat over me. They divide my garments among them and cast lots for my clothing."

Likely the clearest prophecy about Jesus is the entire 53rd chapter of Isaiah. Isaiah 53:3-7 is especially unmistakable: "He was despised and rejected by men, a man of sorrows, and familiar with suffering. Like one from whom men hide their faces he was despised, and we esteemed him not. Surely, he took up our infirmities and carried our sorrows, yet we considered him stricken by God, smitten by him, and afflicted. But he was pierced for our transgressions, he was crushed for our iniquities; the punishment that brought us peace was upon him, and by his wounds we are healed. We all, like sheep, have gone astray, each of us has turned to his own way; and the LORD has laid on him the iniquity of us all. He was oppressed and afflicted, yet he did not open his mouth; he was led like a lamb to the slaughter, and as a sheep before her shearers is silent, so he did not open his mouth."

The "seventy sevens" prophecy in Daniel Chapter 9 predicted the precise date that Jesus, the Messiah, would be "cut off." Isaiah 50:6 accurately describes the beating that Jesus endured. Zechariah 12:10 predicts the "piercing" of the Messiah, which occurred after Jesus died on the cross.

When He finally came, through His miraculous birth, Jesus fulfilled the three main wishes of His Father in Heaven. His death and resurrection guaranteed our wealth, health and holiness. All generations to come will be partakers of the great sacrifice made by Jesus, the Father of divine purpose.

Mary Mother of Jesus

Mary, the mother of Jesus, is the best-known female character in the Bible. We are first introduced to Mary when her name appears in the genealogy of Jesus in the Gospel of Matthew where she is referred to as the wife of Joseph. Though her first mention is in this context, she soon became known as a godly young woman who God chose to carry his Son to term. Mary was the mother of Jesus Christ.

In the time that Mary lived, girls were not always trained in the Holy Scriptures, but were trained mainly to run the home. But Mary evidently had a been trained in the Scriptures.

As seen by her praise of God in her "Magnificat" in Luke 1:47–55, Mary was well-versed in the Scriptures and had hidden portions of it in her heart.

Mary was engaged to Joseph and in that era the engagement, or betrothal, was binding and could only be dissolved by a legal divorce. This engagement was signed by an official and came at least a year before the marriage took place. It is believed that Mary was quite young when she married. Though she was young, and probably poor, Mary had something priceless inside: she was a woman of faith who loved God deeply, having an obedient spirit. Have you ever wondered what kind of woman God would choose to carry His Son? She was chosen to love and nurture Him as her firstborn and raise Him in the knowledge of God.

* Mary was a chaste virgin. In Isaiah 7:14, the prophet Isaiah stated that the Messiah (God's Son) would be born of a virgin. Mary fit the bill. She was a young, unmarried woman; pure and godly.
* Mary was a humble woman. Mary was a small-town girl from the insignificant village of Nazareth. Though she was of nobility, being in the line of King David, the family had lost all its status because of the years of Israel's

captivity and years of foreign domination. No, Mary was a peasant girl, not a princess.

* Mary was an obedient follower. God does not look at outward appearances, but always looks at the heart (1 Samuel 16:7). When God looked at Mary, He saw an obedient woman who would live according to His will, just like her ancestor, David (Acts 13:22)
* Mary was a faithful Jew. Mary was of the tribe of Judah and the line of David. She worshipped the one true God and she knew the Holy Scriptures.

After the birth of Jesus, many curious events occurred. The shepherds, who were out in the fields tending their sheep, had seen angels who told them that their Saviour had just been born and that they should go find the Child in Bethlehem. They found Him and they worshiped. Later, wise men from the East came to Bethlehem to honour the Child, whose "star was seen in the East (Matthew 2:2). They found Him, and they worshiped. Mary just took it all in and she pondered these things in her heart (Luke 2:19). She was given a great responsibility, yes. But she was also given a tremendous gift.

Mary's service to God did not end that first Christmas when Jesus was born. Mary mothered Jesus for the thirty years that he lived with her their poor Nazareth home. From childhood to manhood, Mary loved and nurtured Jesus as he grew into manhood. She did all the things a devoted mother did for the son she knew was no ordinary man. Mary could not surround her Son with wealth. The family was so poor that when she went to the Temple to present Him to the Lord, she could only offer a pair of pigeons - the offering of the very poor. She could not introduce Him to the culture of the day. Being poor and enduring a forced exile in Egypt (Matthew 2:13-15) Mary and Joseph had little education to pass on to the young Jesus. But Mary had so much to give Jesus. She gave him gifts of infinite more value than secular and material advantages.

* She gave Him birth.
* She, along with Joseph, gave him a home.

★ She cultivated in the home a purity of heart, obedience, and love.

Mary was a woman who was blessed by God. Though she seemingly had nothing to offer, she was chosen by God himself to be a part of His plan of redemption of mankind. She was young, poor, and unknown. She had never been a mother, she possessed no wealth or family inheritance, and she boasted no fame or social status. Yet she has been honoured throughout all history for her faithful obedience to God.

Joseph Father of Jesus

God chose Joseph to be the earthly father of Jesus. The Bible tells us in the Gospel of Matthew, that Joseph was a righteous man. His actions toward Mary, his wife-to-be, revealed he was a kind and sensitive man. When Mary told Joseph she was pregnant, he had every right to feel disgraced. He knew the child was not his own, and Mary's apparent unfaithfulness carried a grave social stigma. Joseph not only had the right to divorce Mary, under Jewish law she could be put to death by stoning.

Although Joseph's initial reaction was to break the engagement, the appropriate thing for a righteous man to do, he treated Mary with extreme kindness. He did not want to cause her further shame, so he decided to act quietly. But God sent an angel to Joseph to verify Mary's story and reassure him that his marriage to her was God's will. Joseph willingly obeyed God, in spite of the public humiliation he would face. Perhaps this noble quality made him God's choice for the Messiah's earthly father.

The Bible does not reveal much detail about Joseph's role as father to Jesus Christ, but we know from Matthew, chapter one, that he was an excellent earthly example of integrity and righteousness. Joseph is last mentioned in Scripture when Jesus was 12 years old. We know that he passed on the carpentry trade to his son and raised him in the Jewish traditions and spiritual observances.

Like his wife, Mary, Joseph's divine purpose was to nurture the Saviour of the whole world, Jesus Christ and he performed it with a "A".

Moses Leads God's People Out of Egypt

Moses was born at a time during the Israeli years of exile in Egypt when all male born children were being killed by the Egyptians. The reason the Egyptians were killing male Israeli children was to weaken the male population and ensure that at no time will there ever be a male population big and strong enough to form an army and rise up in resistance against the Egyptians. We see how God engineers the life of Moses to prepare him towards his divine purpose of liberating the Israelis from slavery.

Although Moses grew up in an Egyptian palace with all the trappings of the life of royals, he knows that his purpose was that of a deliverer and when the time to fulfil that mission came, he departed from the palace into the wilderness and helped mount the resistance against Pharaoh. Through many trials and temptations, plagues and all he finally gathered the Israelites and led them across the red sea through the desert into the Promised Land.

Solomon Builder of The Temple Vs David

David was a man after God's heart and graces us with many psalms to show his love and fellowship as he was divinely inspired to write. David started out very wonderfully in life, loved God and pursued the things of God. As a little boy he went to bring food to his brothers when he heard Goliath the Philistine insulting the army of God. With a sling he slew Goliath and saved the Israeli army who were already intimidated by Goliath's boisterous talks.

David walked with God but somewhere along the line so many things happened. He married many wives, committed adultery and murder by placing the husband of the object of his love at the forefront of battle so he would be killed. David was concerned that while he lived in a house, the Tabernacle of God had to be carried around in tents. But God disqualified David and told him there had been too much bloodshed under his reign so instead the building of the Temple was delegated to Solomon his son. It was Solomon's divine assignment to build the first temple. It took Solomon 7 years to build the temple before it was finally dedicated to God. Although it was David's heart desire to build a temple for God to dwell in, God decided to give the assignment to his son Solomon.

When the Temple was completed, Solomon inaugurated it with prayer and sacrifice, and even invited non-Jewish to come and pray there. He urged God to pay particular heed to their prayers: "Thus all the peoples of the earth will know Your name and revere You, as does Your people Israel; and they will recognize that Your name is attached to this House that I have built" (I Kings 8:43).

Solomon thus fulfilled his divine purpose by erecting a temple for God.

John the Baptist, Forerunner of Jesus

Eight hundred years before Christ came, the prophet Isaiah prophesied about his coming. Isaiah also prophesied that there would be a voice of someone crying in the wilderness. This he spoke of John the Baptist who would usher in the earthly ministry of Jesus Christ.

John's divine purpose was to prepare the way for Jesus. Even though he was a prophet in his own right, and baptised people with the so-called baptism of John, he clearly stated that he was not even fit to untie the laces of the sandals of the one who was coming after him. He also prepared the minds of the people to know that there was a higher baptism than that of water which was the baptism in the Holy Ghost which only Jesus could perform.

"I indeed baptize you with water unto repentance. But he that cometh after me is mightier than I, whose shoes I am not worthy to bear: he shall baptize you with the Holy Ghost, and with fire: Whose fan is in his hand, and he will thoroughly purge his floor, and gather his wheat into the garner; but he will burn up the chaff with unquenchable fire." (Mathew 3:11-12)

It is strange that though Jesus was greater than John the Baptist, He still went to be baptised by John. It is during this baptism that the heavens opened and the Holy Spirit descended in the form of a dove and sat on Jesus' head, thereby confirming His divinity and confirming the start of His ministry. With the baptism of Jesus Christ, John the Baptist fulfilled his mission on earth and from thence people's eyes were turned towards following Jesus the Messiah.

Contemporary Examples of People Who Fulfilled Their Purpose

An erroneous belief that often runs in Christian circles is that divine purpose can only be fulfilled by Christians or Christian leaders. In Chapter 1, I mentioned under "Purpose Vs Religion" how Dr Creflo Dollar challenged talk show host Larry King, telling him that he had not found his divine purpose.

We need to approach the subject of other people's contribution to the Kingdom of God with so much delicacy. If John, an atheist, discovers the television and Susan later uses it to preach the gospel, can it not be said that John fulfilled a divine purpose of creating a tool for the expansion of God's Kingdom? It is easy to look out for the obvious:

"But God hath chosen the foolish things of the world to confound the wise; and God hath chosen the weak things of the world to confound the things which are mighty; And base things of the world, and things which are despised, hath God

chosen, yea, and things which are not, to bring to nought things that are: That no flesh should glory in his presence".
(1 Corinthians 1:27-29).

Dr Miles Munroe and the Pursuit of Purpose

One of God's children in our time that really fulfilled his divine purpose was the late Dr Miles Munroe. His focus in ministry was to steer people into finding their true place in the world. So passionate was he about the need to find purpose that he once said: *"The greatest tragedy in life is not death, but life without a reason".*

Myles Munroe, OBE (20 April 1954 – 9 November 2014) was a Bahamian evangelist and ordained minister avid professor of the Kingdom of God, author, speaker and leadership consultant who founded and led the Bahamas Faith Ministries International (BFMI) and Myles Munroe International (MMI). He was chief executive officer and chairman of the board of the International Third World Leaders Association and president of the International Leadership Training Institute as well as the author of numerous books.

Born Myles Egbert Munroe in 1954 in Nassau, Bahamas, Munroe grew up poor in a family of eleven children. Raised in the Nassau suburb of Bain Town, he was a life-long resident of the Commonwealth. Munroe became a Christian during his teenage years, later attending Oral Roberts University (ORU) where he received his Bachelor of Fine Arts, Education, and Theology in 1978 and a Master's degree in administration from the University of Tulsa in 1980. Munroe was also the recipient of honorary doctoral degrees from various schools of higher education and served as an adjunct professor of the Graduate School of Theology at ORU.

Dr Miles Munroe is a prolific writer on several Kingdom subjects but he is well known for his work on finding your purpose. He has written way too many books to mention here but here are some of his books.

- The Pursuit of Purpose
- Understanding the Purpose and Power of Men
- Understanding the Purpose and Power of Woman
- Purpose and Power of Love and Marriage
- Unleash Your Purpose

Here are some principles he espoused about fulfilling divine purpose.

Tell your story: He argued that until you can be bold in expressing yourself, the world will never be a partaker of your divine purpose.

Speak the original truth to others: All he did was tell us the original truth about who we are and who God is. The Kingdom message resonates with your spirit when you hear it because it reminds us that we were born for something bigger than ourselves. So, our goal is to encourage others to cancel all excuses and get them to believe that they can do what they were born to do." Dr Munroe said: "When you latch on to what God says about you and reject the naysayers, you don't toil in life. You become so focused on your purpose and passion it protects you from needlessly expending energy in areas outside of God's will. It really upsets me when I see people in this state because if they only knew the truth, they would be set free."

Leadership is self-discovery: "When you become yourself, automatically you become a leader. We all have the potential, but you can't just decide to be a leader...you have to become you or better yet God's original idea of you. Sadly, most people die as followers because they never discover who they are, their purpose or potential. Leadership in its simplicity is the self-discovery process."

Don't toil in life: Dr Miles Munroe said, "When you latch on to what God says about you and reject the naysayers, you don't toil in life. You become so focused on your purpose and passion it protects you from needlessly expending energy in areas outside of God's will. It really upsets me when I see people in this state because if they only knew the truth, they would be set free."

Generational problem solving: "Your purpose will solve a problem that your generation needs, but first you have to take the steps of: becoming yourself, discovering your purpose, identity, who you are and writing out your life vision. This is the formula for success and once you do this...then you become influential and start getting people's attention."

Dr Munroe also believes that:

- Purpose gives confidence
- Purpose provides protection
- Purpose empowers perseverance
- Purpose introduces and maintains objectivity
- Purpose sustains contentment
- Purpose creates joy
- Purpose brings the intercession of the Holy Spirit.

His work on finding and fulfilling purpose is greatly appreciated and he will be sorely missed.

Don Moen and Worship

You would be hard pressed to find any Christian that does not know a Don Moen song. Don is a glaring example of divine purpose manifestation and his life deserves mention in this book.

Donald James "Don" Moen (Born June 29, 1950) is an American singer-songwriter, pastor, and producer of Christian worship music.

Before Moen was hired to work for Integrity Music, he attended Oral Roberts University and became a Living Sound musician for Terry Law Ministries and travelled with Terry Law for ten years. He produced 11 volumes for the Hosanna! Music series of worship albums. His first album under his own name, Worship with Don Moen, was released in 1992. His music has total global sales of over five million units.

Moen worked for Integrity Media for over 20 years, serving as creative director and president of Integrity Music, president of Integrity Label Group, and an executive producer of Integrity Music albums. He left Integrity Media in December 2007 to start a new initiative, The Don Moen Company. The Don Moen Company acquired MediaComplete, the church software company that created MediaShout. Moen became a radio host for Don Moen & Friends in 2009. Moen received a Dove Award for his work on the musical God with Us in addition to nine nominations for his songs.

Moen also worked with Claire Cloninger, Paul Overstreet, Martin J. Nystrom, Randy Rothwell, Ron Kenoly, Bob Fitts, Debbye Graafsma, Paul Baloche, Tom Brooks, among many others. He worked with musicians, Justo Almario, Carl Albrecht, Abraham Laboriel, Alex Acuna, Paul Jackson, Jr., Lenny LeBlanc and Chris Graham. He was a catalyst in launching the careers of Paul Baloche, Darlene Zschech, Israel Houghton, and Hillsong United.[5]

Ask Don Moen what he does, and the answer might surprise you. He won't say he's a songwriter even though he's written more than 100 songs. He won't say he's a worship leader even though he's led worship on every continent but Antarctica and recorded numerous albums. He won't say he's a businessman or producer even though he has produced and directed hundreds of successful projects. If you ask Don Moen why God put him on this planet, he'll tell you, "To be an architect who designs products and events that help people experience God's presence in a new and fresh way." And in more than three decades of ministry, he's had lots of opportunity to fulfil that purpose. His discography reflects his passion to create resources for the church that lead people into an honest and intimate relationship with the Lord. In 2002, his peers recognized that lifelong commitment and presented him with the Ray DeVries Church Ministry Award.

Don has also received a Dove Award for his work on the musical "God With Us" and has received multiple Dove Award nominations for his songs, CDs and choral resources. In addition to his writing and recording, Don makes time to tour domestically and abroad and has performed with artists such as Leanne Albright, Chris Tomlin, Twila Paris, Sara Groves and Paul Baloche, to name a few. He also has served as worship leader for past National Day of Prayer events and as a music industry spokesperson, having been featured on Fox News, NPR and in USA Today.

Don is as popular overseas as he is at home in the U.S. His travels for concerts and seminars have taken him to Ghana, South Africa, Singapore, the Philippines, South Korea, Brazil, Canada, Australia, Great Britain, Hong Kong, Malaysia, Indonesia, Japan, Guatemala, Honduras, and elsewhere. Today, Don is President of Don Moen Productions in Nashville, Tennessee, where he resides with his wife Laura and five children.

It became very clear to Don when he met a little girl named Gifty in Accra, Ghana, that God wanted him to do more than just sing and lead people into worship. God wanted Don to step out and be Christ's hands and feet to hurting people. The purpose of Worship In Action is to do just that: to be the tangible hands and feet of Christ to people who have lost hope.

Bill Gates and Computers

William Henry Gates III popularly known as Bill Gates, was born on 28 October 1955. He is an American business giant and co-founder of Microsoft which has graced billions of homes with the wonder machine we call computers. As CEO and Chief Software Architect of Microsoft from 1975 until about 2006, Bill gates has contributed a lot to humanity in the field of artificial intelligence. We can all agree that computers have changed the whole world of education, business, science, medicine and even the gospel. Although the widespread use of computers has brought with it many challenges that the world must deal with, we are unanimous in the fact that 21st century life has been made much easier by the advent of computers.

Moved by a passion to help the world, Bill Gates has all but withdrawn from active work in Microsoft to form The Bill and Melinda Gates foundation to promote charitable work around the world. In 2009 Bill Gates and Warren Buffet founded The Giving Pledge where other billionaires pledged to give 50% or more of their wealth to charitable causes around the world. Bill and Melinda Gates have pledged $100 million to the fight against HIV, the pandemic that has claimed millions of lives on all continents worldwide. Their dedication to AIDS research that will help reduce the transmission of the disease will go a long way to help people on every part of the globe.

Time Magazine has listed Bill Gates among the 100 of the most influential people of the 20th century. He has given out grants, scholarships and supported charitable projects all over the world. He has invested in the International Rice Research Institute which is developing the so-called Golden Rice a genetically manipulated rice that can be used to combat vitamin A deficiency.

Bill and Melinda have received several awards from all over the world, honorary degrees, Doctorates and has even been Knighted by Queen Elizabeth II, all in recognition of their philanthropic work and service to humanity. Now being the richest man in the world and an astute business man has won him many controversies as well but if his only purpose on earth was to put a computer on our tables, he has done a good job so far. Bill and Melinda Gates are dedicated to helping in the eradication and fight against diseases such as childhood polio, which has seen the crippling and death of many children worldwide. To both, their wealth is a tool for the betterment of the world.

> "My wife and I had a long dialogue about how we were going to take the wealth that we're lucky enough to have and give it back in a way that's most impactful to the world," he says. "Both of us worked at Microsoft and saw that if you

take innovation and smart people, the ability to measure what's working, that you can pull together some pretty dramatic things. "We're focused on the help of the poorest in the world, which really drives you into vaccination. You can actually take a disease and get rid of it altogether, like we are doing with polio."

Mother Teresa of Calcutta and Charity

Although most of the world only knows Mother Teresa in relation to India, she is originally from Kosovo. She was born under the name Anjezë Gonxhe Bojaxhiu in Skopje Kosovo on the 26th of August 1910. Mother Teresa, who was recently canonized by the Catholic church and named Saint Teresa of Calcutta was an Albanian-Indian nun and Catholic missionary, who dedicated her life and service to the poor on the streets of Calcutta in India. After living in her home country for 18 years, she moved to Ireland and then to India where she spent the rest of her life.

Mother Teresa was a teacher for many years in India before she received what is known as "The call within a call". Being a nun meant that she had already accepted a call of "chastity, celibacy and poverty" in service of God and the catholic church. She said of herself:

> *"By blood, I am Albanian. By citizenship, I am an Indian. By faith, I am a Catholic nun. As to my calling, I belong to the world. As to my heart, I belong entirely to the Heart of Jesus."*

It was during her life and service in India that she received a distinct calling from the Lord as she described it. She said Jesus spoke to her and told her to abandon her teaching to work in the slums of Calcutta helping the city's poorest and sickest people. Even though she enjoyed teaching she had often wondered at the abject poverty and misery on the streets of Calcutta. Mother Teresa was an ardent pro-life ambassador and even though she was criticised by many for her tough stance against abortion, I believe strongly that many more babies were saved because the poor preferred to carry their pregnancy to term and abandon them in the safe baby bins provided or dumped on the streets where they could be found. She founded The Missionaries of Charity Religious Order which carried out numerous charitable duties on the streets of India. Mother Teresa championed adoption as a solution to abortion, claiming that there was no reason why a child should be aborted when there were millions of childless couples willing to adopt these children.

Together with the other sisters in the Missionary of Charity Community, they founded homes for the elderly, orphanages and schools for street children. They also catered for refugees, prostitutes, lepers, the mentally ill, AIDS sufferers and many more people abandoned by society. All these services were carried out free of charge. Together with the other volunteers, they brought hope to the city of Calcutta. Mother Teresa is fondly remembered worldwide by Catholics, non-Catholics, Christians and non-Christians, politicians and the world at large. She received the Nobel Peace Prize in 1979 for her service to humanity. Her divine purpose was to serve the poorest of the poor and she did that all her life and died among them in Calcutta. Her death shook the catholic community and the world at large and she remains an icon of service to humanity. Hers is a purpose led life worth emulating.

Thomas Edison and the Light Bulb

It is hard for most people today — at least those of us in so-called "developed countries" — to remember or even imagine a world without telephones, movie theaters, recorded music or even electric lights. But that was the world when Thomas Edison was born in 1847. Edison literally gave expression to God's declaration "let there be light"!

By his early twenties, he had already registered patents on several of his own inventions, and sold the rights to an improved stock ticker, making him wealthy. He was now in a position to explore any field he wanted.

Over the next few years, he continued to invent and patent a number of successful inventions. One of the most successful was a new carbon microphone which finally made Alexander Bell's new "telephone" device loud enough and clear enough for practical use. (This same technology was still widely used in telephones right up to the 1980s.)

His wide-ranging curiosity took his research in many directions. For example, in 1877, he invented the phonograph...a way of recording voices and music onto fragile wax cylinders. This new technology so amazed and excited the public imagination that Edison became immediately famous for it.

But a year later he began the search for a practical, reliable form of electric lighting. In truth, Edison didn't actually even "invent" the light bulb; a number of other inventors had developed forms of electric lighting before he began his experiments. He simply found a better material (carbonized thread) to use as the filament. No, his real achievement was far bigger: making electric light commercially practical.

Because before his new bulb would do anyone any good, Edison had to invent an entire electrical distribution system that could support city-sized populations.

Four years, from the first successful light bulb in a laboratory to the first generating station, Edison started supplying 85 customers in New York City. And after that, the growth was exponential: one year later, he had 550 customers, with almost 11,000 electric lights, and was opening a second generating station. He had also established Edison companies to handle each part of the electricity supply chain.

He immediately went on to develop some of the first motion picture technologies, producing not just the equipment or the projectors, but also the content, in the form of hundreds of short films.

Once again, he had to invent (and patent!) every link in the chain. And once again he managed to find huge success in the process. Edison's name became almost synonymous with sound recordings and motion pictures in the early years of the 20th century.

It is no coincidence that Apple followed the Edison "own the whole chain" model when they rolled out the world-changing iPhone and iTunes. Edison has always been one of Steve Jobs' heroes.

Edison said of himself: *"I never quit until I get what I'm after. Negative results are just what I'm after. They are just as valuable to me as positive results"*.

Thomas Edison showed us that if you treat every result as a positive result, then you set yourself up for success. If that is your mindset, you literally cannot fail.

Martin Luther King and the Civil Rights Movement

The second child of Martin Luther King Sr. (1899-1984), a pastor, and Alberta Williams King (1904-1974), a former schoolteacher, Martin Luther King Jr. was born in Atlanta, Georgia, on January 15, 1929.

A gifted student, King attended segregated public schools and at the age of 15 was admitted to Morehouse College, the alma mater of both his father and maternal grandfather, where he studied medicine and law. After graduating in 1948, King entered Crozer Theological Seminary in Pennsylvania, where he earned a Bachelor of Divinity degree, won a prestigious fellowship and was elected president of his predominantly white senior class.

King then enrolled in a graduate program at Boston University, completing his coursework in 1953 and earning a doctorate in systematic theology two years later. While in Boston he met Coretta Scott (1927-2006), a young singer from Alabama who was studying at the New England Conservatory of Music. The couple wed in 1953 and settled in Montgomery, Alabama, where King became pastor of the Dexter Avenue Baptist Church. They had four children: Yolanda Denise King (1955-2007), Martin Luther King III (born 1957), Dexter Scott King (born 1961) and Bernice Albertine King (born 1963).

The King family had been living in Montgomery for less than a year when the highly segregated city became the epicentre of the burgeoning struggle for civil rights in America, galvanized by the landmark Brown v. Board of Education of Topeka decision of 1954. On December 1, 1955, Rosa Parks (1913-2005), secretary of the local National Association for the Advancement of Coloured People chapter, refused to give up her seat to a white passenger on a Montgomery bus and was arrested. Activists coordinated a bus boycott that would continue for 381 days, placing a severe economic strain on the public transit system and downtown business owners. They chose Martin Luther King Jr. as the protest's leader and official spokesman.

By the time the Supreme Court ruled segregated seating on public buses unconstitutional in November 1956, King, heavily influenced by Mahatma Gandhi (1869-1948) and the activist Bayard Rustin (1912-1987), had entered the national spotlight as an inspirational proponent of organized, nonviolent resistance. (He had also become a target for white supremacists, who firebombed his family home that January.) Emboldened by the boycott's success, in 1957 he and other civil rights activists—most of them fellow ministers—founded the Southern Christian Leadership Conference (SCLC), a group committed to achieving full equality for African Americans through nonviolence. (Its motto was "Not one hair of one head of one person should be harmed.") He would remain at the helm of this influential organization until his death.

In his role as SCLC president, Martin Luther King Jr. travelled across the country and around the world, giving lectures on nonviolent protest and civil rights as well as meeting with religious figures, activists and political leaders.

In 1960 King and his family moved to Atlanta, his native city, where he joined his father as co-pastor of the Ebenezer Baptist Church. Later that year, Martin Luther King Jr. worked with a number of civil rights and religious groups to organize the March on Washington for Jobs and Freedom, a peaceful political rally designed to shed light on the injustices African Americans continued to face across the country. Held on August 28 and attended by some 200,000 to 300,000 participants, the event is widely regarded as a watershed moment in the history of the American civil rights movement and a factor in the passage of the Civil Rights Act of 1964.

The march culminated in King's most famous address, known as the "I Have a Dream" speech, a spirited call for peace and equality that many consider a masterpiece of rhetoric. Standing on the steps of the Lincoln Memorial–a monument to the president who a century earlier had brought down the institution of slavery in the United States—he shared his vision of a future in which "this nation will rise up and live out the true meaning of its creed: 'We hold these truths to be self-evident, that all men are created equal.'" The speech and march cemented King's reputation at home and abroad; later that year he was named Man of the Year by TIME magazine and in 1964 became the youngest person ever awarded the Nobel Peace Prize.

In the spring of 1965, King's elevated profile drew international attention to the violence that erupted between white segregationists and peaceful demonstrators in Selma, Alabama, where the SCLC and Student Nonviolent Coordinating Committee (SNCC) had organized a voter registration campaign. Captured on television, the brutal scene outraged many Americans and inspired supporters from across the country to gather in Selma and take part in a march to Montgomery led by King and supported by President

Lyndon Johnson (1908-1973), who sent in federal troops to keep the peace. That August, Congress passed the Voting Rights Act, which guaranteed the right to vote.

On the evening of April 4, 1968, King was fatally shot while standing on the balcony of a motel in Memphis, where he had travelled to support a sanitation workers' strike. In the wake of his death, a wave of riots swept major cities across the country, while President Johnson declared a national day of mourning.

After years of campaigning by activists, members of Congress and Coretta Scott King, among others, in 1983 President Ronald Reagan (1911-2004) signed a bill creating a U.S. federal holiday in honour of King. Observed on the third Monday of January, it was first celebrated in 1986.

Although King's life was short, he fulfilled his divine purpose of fighting for the equality of God's children first in America, then around the world. Some of us in his privileged position would have kept our privileges and shunned the fight for civil liberties. King paid the ultimate price while fulfilling his divine calling.

Henry Ford and The Ford Automobile

Henry Ford's parents left Ireland during the potato famine and settled in the Detroit area in the 1840s. Ford was born in what is now Dearborn, Michigan. His formal education was limited, but even as a youngster, he was handy with machinery. He worked for the Detroit Edison company, advancing from machine-shop apprentice to chief engineer. In 1893, Ford built a gasoline engine, and within a few years, an automobile, still a novelty item of the rich or do-it-yourself engineers.

At the beginning of the 20th century the automobile was a plaything for the rich. Most models were complicated machines that required a chauffeur conversant with its individual mechanical nuances to drive it. Henry Ford was determined to build a simple, reliable and affordable car; a car the average American worker could afford. Out of this determination came the Model T and the assembly line - two innovations that revolutionized American society and moulded the world we live in today.

Henry Ford did not invent the car; he produced an automobile that was within the economic reach of the average American. While other manufacturers were content to target a market of the well-to-do, Ford developed a design and a method of manufacture that would make the car affordable to the ordinary American. Henry Ford founded his first car the Quadricycle, which he built in 1896, steadily reducing the cost of the Model T. Instead of pocketing the profits; Ford lowered the price of his car. As a result, Ford Motors sold more cars and steadily increased its earnings - transforming the automobile from a luxury toy to a mainstay of American society.

The Model T made its debut in 1908 with a purchase price of $825.00. Over ten thousand were sold in its first year, establishing a new record. Four years later the price dropped to $575.00 and sales soared. By 1914, Ford could claim a 48% share of the automobile market.

Central to Ford's ability to produce an affordable car was the development of the assembly line that increased the efficiency of manufacture and decreased its cost. Ford did not conceive the concept, he perfected it. Prior to the introduction of the assembly line, cars were individually crafted by teams of skilled workmen - a slow and expensive procedure. The assembly line reversed the process of automobile manufacture. Instead of workers going to the car, the car came to the worker who performed the same task of assembly over and over again. With the introduction and perfection of the process, Ford was able to reduce the assembly time of a Model T from twelve and a half hours to less than six hours.

Henry Ford had a very large impact on the way we live today. The Henry Ford Heritage Association feels his stamp on our lives is real and significant. The consumer ethic and middle-class lifestyle we live today are heralded around the world as the American way of life.

That lifestyle has its roots in Henry Ford. His desire to build a product everyone could use and afford resulted in a transformative seed change that was felt around the world. His desire to pay his workers a wage that could do more than sustain their existence brought a whole new economic class into being. His concern for worker's wellbeing went beyond their pay envelope and that concern helped to define employer/employee relations and benefits which are with us to this day.

Ford has enabled so many to drive cars and move around freely. The Fiesta has officially become the best-selling car of all time in Britain with Ford announcing it has shifted 4,115,000 in the last 38 years.

The fact that people can move freely from place to place and fulfil their vision by dint of cars, including Ford models, is proof that Henry Ford fulfilled his divine purpose.

CHAPTER 10

THE ROLE OF PURPOSE HELPERS AND PURPOSE KILLERS

> "Be not deceived: evil companions corrupt
> good morals". 1 Corinthians 15:33

THE WAY GOD created man, is for him not to be an island living in isolation and doing everything like a hermit locked up in some ecological paradise. Man is a social being and relies on other human beings as well as other elements of God's creation to fulfil his God given purpose. If human beings had to rely solely on themselves and their personal abilities to fulfil all the tasks they have to accomplish, God would have to create super beings. But we live in interdependence, hence the need for purpose helpers.

Conversely, as we set out to fulfil our divine purpose, not all those that surround us mean well and we need to be vigilant and detect purpose killers.

Divine Purpose Helpers

The first step towards working with God is finding the everyday little tasks we need to be working on towards fulfilling our divine purpose. But a very important factor is to recognize and utilise the services and input of purpose helpers.

Purpose helpers are catalysts of divine purpose. They are the people and things that God puts in our path to help us carry out the task that is set before us. As a midwife is there to help women bring babies safely into the world, these helpers are there to provide the necessary support we need to fulfil our divine purpose. When God places a divine assignment in your hands, it is of utmost importance that you find out and recognise the people God has placed in your path to be part of the delivery process.

Wives and Husbands as Purpose Helpers

As a Christian and as a pastor it is with pain that I leave counselling sessions between men and women of God who have clearly not found the role they need to play in each other's lives as they each struggle to fulfil Gods purpose. When Christians are courting you find them saying things like "I like a man who loves God". "I like a man who serves God". "I like a woman who is passionate about serving God……" However, many years down the marriage lane, these same pursuits have sadly become the most latent source of conflict between couples in ministry.

When you are in ministry it is very important to understand the role, you play in the calling of your spouse. A great understanding of this principle is found in the book of Genesis 2:18, when God created Adam in the Garden of Eden. He said, "And the Lord God said, *"It is not good that the man should be alone; I will make him an help meet for him"*. God recognised that the task he had placed before Adam, would require a helper who was meet for him. The lion in all its ferocity could not be Adam's helper, the elephant with its mammoth size could not cut it, neither could the flowers in all their splendour fulfil that role.

A spouse must explore and understand the role they need to play. And let's get one thing straight a role can be active or passive, supporting or interactive. Let me give a typical example. If a doctor is married to a nurse the level of career and professional interaction and interdependence between the two will be much higher than if the doctor was married to a cook or a landscape gardener. Many ministers' homes have collapsed because the spouse did not understand the role they were supposed to be carrying out in the partner's divine purpose.

When God gives you an assignment, He will put in your way the people He will use to help you fulfil it. It is heart breaking when as a minister of the gospel. I see wonderful Christian homes destroyed on the very alter of divine purpose and service. I hear things like "Pastor he has no time for me.", "He has no time for his family", "He is a stranger to the kids. He loves the church more than he loves us." And you will hear the man saying: "This is my calling, when you married me you knew that it was part of the package, so you have to deal with it. You don't have the same passion for this call as I do. You are too carnal".

If it falls your lot to help your spouse fulfil their divine purpose, help them to the best of your ability. Conversely, if you discover your spouse does not understand what they need to do, help them along gently.

Ecclesiastes 4: 9-10 says:

> "Two are better than one; because they have a good reward for their labour. For if they fall, the one will lift up his fellow: but woe to him that is alone when he falleth; for he hath not another to help him up".

Jesus and the 12 Apostles

When Jesus Christ came to the earth, He was God Himself incarnate. He had a divine purpose he wanted to fulfil. His first destiny helpers were his earthly parents, Mary his mother for being a vessel which God used for Him to enter into this world and be nursed by her. Then His father Joseph for being the best foster father a child could dream of. When his childhood days were over, and he had to start his ministry, the first thing he did was recruit his purpose helpers in the person of the 12 Apostles.

If Jesus, God incarnate, needed helpers to aid him in his earthly journey, how much more do we mere mortals, need to surround ourselves with people who will help us fulfil our calling. Need I also mention that apart from the 12 disciples, Jesus had many other men and women who helped him in his earthly ministry. Some followed him from town to town, helping to minister to him and his disciples and the people who came to hear him preach. Together they toured the cities and its environs ministering to people daily. On his own, Jesus would not have been able to do all that work. Just imagine the feeding of the 5000 episode. Jesus would have had to preach the word, find them a comfortable place, find food to feed all of the 5000, distribute the food, collect leftovers and tend to the children. This is a mammoth task for one individual to accomplish without any help.

Ministers today need helpers to avoid the burnout syndrome. I visited a church once and after the service I felt sorry for the pastor. He was the pastor, the choir leader, the guitarist, the keyboardist and the announcer all at the same. Do not get me wrong this pastor was evidently a multi-talented person, he could sing, preach, play the guitar as well as the keyboard. During worship, he led one or two songs with the guitar then took it off to sit down and play the piano for subsequent songs and then woke up again to continue. Mike up mike down, screw here unscrew there, tighten here, loosen there, shuffle chairs here and there and so on. After a hectic praise and worship session, he was back on the pulpit sweating profusely to deliver a 25-minute sermon. Lord have mercy was all I could cry!

He was very talented no doubt about it but I shook my head as I wondered how long he would be able to keep all that up. At the beginning of a ministry when there are few people this can be endured but as a ministry grows the leader should gradually recruit and relinquish tasks to his purpose helpers. You can't be a do-it-all even if you are a know-it-all. God gave you only two hands and two legs for a reason otherwise he would have made you an octopus.

The Church Family as Purpose Helpers

In a typical church environment, you have many different people functioning in different capacities including the choir, the sound technicians, the ushers, the prayer department and the church elders. These various departments work together to ensure a smooth and effective running of the ministry.

As I mentioned above about my fellow pastor friend, the church family exists for a reason.; your natural family exists for a reason; your friends and your peer groups exist for a purpose; your work colleagues, your spouse and your children are all individual stepping stones that God has placed on your path to help you accomplish your calling.

Sometimes the mistake that we as pastors and spiritual leaders make is acknowledging those who serve in various outstanding positions and inadvertently forget to recognise those who serve in many other low-key positions.

We are co-labourers in the divine vineyard.

Teachers as Purpose Helpers

We may not all readily accept, understand or see the role that teachers play in life purpose but they do play a vital role. By teachers I mean academic, secular and spiritual teachers. People who act and fall into different categories including, elders, mums, dads, grandparents, big brothers, big sisters, counsellors and mentors.

In life, it is one thing to know your life's purpose yet it is another ball game altogether to learn and understand and gain the knowledge and experience you need to fulfil your divine purpose. Teachers are those who painstakingly give us the building stones needed to fulfil our calling. Teachers are some of the most despised people in the world yet the most impactful. Most people still have fond memories of their favourite teachers as well as bitter memories of cruel ones. Some teachers would make learning such a pleasurable experience while others would be task masters. All of this tends to affect the level and quality of execution of our divine purpose.

In the craftsmanship industry in the days past such as carpentry, plumbing, building and masonry, to learn a trade, the trainee had to enlist the services of a master in the art of his choice and go and sit under his tutelage for a certain period and be taught all that they needed to know to provide the required standard of service demanded in that industry. In many cases the mentee had to live with the master craftsman during his tutelage.

To fulfil your divine purpose, you need to identify teachers and mentors that will help you on the journey that is ahead of you.

There are many other examples of destiny helpers in the scriptures.

Elijah, Elisha and the Widow of Zarephath

Elijah is one of the well-known Old Testament prophets of the nation of Israel. His name means "God is Jehovah" and he is one of the greatest of the prophets. When you speak of Elijah the first story that comes to mind is the duel at Mount Carmel with the prophets of Baal. We first met Elijah in 1 Kings 17:1 where he challenged the evil king Ahab and prophesied drought upon the land. Out of fear he fled to the brook of Cherith where he was fed by ravens. This was God's own way of setting Elijah apart from the impurity and evil that was going on in the land at that time. But because there was drought in the land, the brook eventually dried up. That is when God sent him to Zarephath to the house of a gentile widow. When he asked for cake and a drink, the widow told Elijah she had none but the last flour and oil in her poverty-stricken home which she intended to prepare their last meal so she and her son could eat and die. Upon Elijah's instruction, she made him a cake and Elijah blessed the widow and her flour and oil were multiplied. Later when the woman's son fell ill and died God used Elijah to bring her son back to life. Here we see the widow being a destiny helper to Elijah and *vice versa*. God had raised the gentile widow to be there to meet Elijah's need during the time of famine.

We next encounter Elijah on Mount Carmel where he challenges the prophets of Baal to an offering of fire contests and commands fire from Heaven. Elijah's purpose was to open the eyes of the people to see that God remains the greatest and in control of the elements. He also wanted to help turn back the heart of the people who had been misled into idol worship and wipe out idolatry. When God sent fire and consumed the offering on Elijah's alter, he validated Elijah's divine purpose:

> *And it came to pass at the time of the offering of the evening sacrifice, that Elijah the prophet came near, and said, LORD God of Abraham, Isaac, and of Israel, let it be known this day that thou art God in Israel, and that I am thy servant, and that I have done all these things at thy word.* 1 Kings 18:36

God send rain to Israel but Elijah fled when he heard that Jezebel, Ahab's wife was plotting to kill him for disgracing her husband King Ahab and all the prophets of Baal. Elijah was afraid and wondered if he was the only true prophet of God left. That is when God told him about the other prophets as well as Elisha who would take his place and carry on with the work of eradicating idol worship in Israel. Elijah came out of hiding and met Elisha and cast his mantle upon him. From then on, a special tutor mentor relationship unfolded between the two. Elisha went back to his family, slew oxen, made a feast and bid his family goodbye. From then on, he followed Elisha wherever he went.

This relationship, displays a very important aspect of our life— the purposeful choosing of friends. Elisha attaches himself to Elijah, imploring the older man not to leave him in 2 Kings 2:2. Responding to Elijah's declaration that he was leaving for Bethel, Elisha exclaimed, *"As the Lord lives, and as you yourself live, I will not leave you."*

Elisha was absolutely devoted to his friend and mentor, because he knew the older man would make an excellent guide.

It is important to choose friends who are wise, focused, passionate about what they do and understand what we are doing. It is often said show me your friend and I will tell you who you are. In bringing himself close to Elijah, Elisha prepared himself for his destiny, finding the mentor and friend who would help him become a worthy prophet and servant of God.

Pharaoh versus Joseph

The first thing that comes to mind when we hear the name Joseph, is dreams. We all know him as Joseph the dreamer whose dreams finally drove a wedge between him and his brothers until he was sold into slavery. Josephs divine assignment was unfolding through all these mishaps. Each temptation took him closer to his divine purpose. I am very sure if we were in Josephs shoes and found ourselves being thrown into a pit and finally sold into slavery by our very own brethren, we would have thought our life was finished. But even in the prison his life had not ended. All his trials and tribulations were pathways to his divine purpose.

Joseph had one divine purpose and that was to help the Egyptians figure out how to handle the oncoming years of famine and, through this position, also save his family and the Israelites from starvation during the great famine. While in prison, he interpreted dreams for his inmates and when Pharaoh had a dream no one could interpret, someone remembered Joseph and he was called in. He gave the interpretation of that dream and earned himself the place of what would be considered today as Prime Minister and second in command of Egypt.

Joseph was a purpose helper to Pharaoh as he helped him rule his country and provide for his subjects during a time of severe famine. Without Joseph in Pharaohs life at this time, all of Egypt may have perished in the famine. Pharaoh was also a purpose helper to Joseph as he lifted him to high office and the grain that was preserved during the years of plenty was enough to feed Egypt and still leave loads leftover to sell to other neighbouring nations and through this, many lives were preserved.

Divine Purpose Killers

It is not possible to talk about destiny helpers without sending out a sound warning about destiny killers. As we carry out our divine assignment we should know and be sensitive to the fact that not everybody that comes our way should be sucked into our journey as we try to fulfil our purpose. Destiney killers can be many different things both animate and inanimate things. A destiny killer can be a person, a thing, a wrong career choice, a bad habit: a wrong friendship etc.

Abraham and Lot

A good example of a destiny killer is a wrong friendship or association. A good example is the relationship between our patriarch of faith father Abraham and his nephew Lot. In the book of Genesis, we read how God called Abraham and asked him to leave his home and move unto a place that he was going to show him.

Now the Lord said to Abram:

> *Now the Lord had said unto Abram, Get thee out of thy country, and from thy kindred, and from thy father's house, unto a land that I will shew thee: And I will make of thee a great nation, and I will bless thee, and make thy name great; and thou shalt be a blessing: And I will bless them that bless thee, and curse him that curses thee: and in thee shall all families of the earth be blessed." (Gen 12: 1-3)*

At no point did God instruct Abraham to take his nephew Lot with him on his journey to Canaan. Yet in Genesis 12 verse four we are told that when Abraham left Haran, he took Lot with him. And as the journey unfolds, we are told how quarrels began to break out between the servants of both men to the extent that they had to part ways at some point during the journey to Canaan.

There was strife between the herdsmen of Abram's livestock and the herdsmen of Lot's livestock. Now the Canaanite and the Perizzite were dwelling then in the land.

So, Abram said to Lot:

> *"Please let there be no strife between you and me, nor between my herdsmen and your herdsmen, for we are brothers. Is not the whole land before you? Please separate from me; if to the left, then I will go to the right; or if to the right, then I will go to the left." (Genesis 13: 7-9)*

If Lot had not come along with Abraham, there would not have been any quarrels and fights on the way to Canaan.

I am a pastor and I can tell you what family feuds can do to a home, a business venture, a church and the wider community. Family feuds have destroyed whole ministries and rendered years of hard work to naught. I am not saying people should not help their families out but be sure that whatever move you make is divinely approved and not a thorn in your flesh you will later seek to get rid of. It would have been okay if it was just the servants that were fighting but we are told that Lot himself was greedy. When Abraham told him to pick out where to go to so that they could avoid their servants quarrelling we are told that when Lot lifted up his eyes and saw the valleys of the Jordan how it had many rivers and springs, meaning that he and his flock will be well catered for, he chose that part of the land and Abraham had to make do with the rest. Lot forgot that it was Abraham who brought him of his accord on the journey and was greedy to take the first pick of the best land.

This example may seem far-fetched to us as we no longer live in an agrarian society but I have a more home-based example. I know of two friends who studied pharmacy in the United Kingdom and graduated together. They decided to open a pharmacy together. One of them re-mortgaged his house and used it as collateral while the other brought only his time and expertise. They both agreed that for three years they would both withdraw only 200 pounds each monthly until the business matured and began to yield greater profit. Before the first half of year two was even up, the second partner was already agitating. He said he was a pharmacist, he wanted to live big and he didn't see why he should postpone living a life of luxury. He pressured the other partner to buy him out and keep his pharmacy and live on 200 pounds if he so wished. Their feuds were so bitter that sometimes workers would hear them exchanging bitter words at the back of the pharmacy and in several instances, it almost got to a physical altercation. While one was dedicated to providing sincere healthcare services to the local community, the other was interested in quick profits, cutting corners and disregarding patient care and National Health guidelines. Painful as it was that is what an otherwise good partnership had come to. They parted ways and the brother who believed in his vision and kept on now owns six pharmacies ten years down the line. The other partner is now unheard of. Such feuds could actually cost people a life time investment from which they may never recover.

This is what greed can cost you. Abraham was lucky that God blessed him wherever he went.

So, as we strive to fulfil our divine purpose, we should carefully and prayerfully handpick those we let into our visionary space to avoid heartache and keep us focused on the mission.

CHAPTER 11

WAIT ON THE LORD AND BE THANKFUL

"He hath made everything beautiful in his time ..."
Ecclesiastes 3:11

IN CHAPTER 10 we saw how our divine purpose may be helped or hindered by people or circumstances. In this chapter, I would like to encourage you to wait on the Lord and be thankful. Your purpose may take time to manifest but while you wait for it, keep doing what you are doing with a thankful heart.

Your Purpose May Take Time

Whatever you set out to do on earth has a gestation period. All the champions of purpose we saw in Chapter 9 did not start fulfilling their purpose overnight. Even the Master Jesus came to the world as a baby and it took him up to 33 years to start His Ministry. Nothing kills divine purpose like impatience.

When you identify your purpose, you need to start mapping out what you would require to manifest it. Habakkuk 2:2-3 is the gold standard for waiting for our purpose or goal:

> *"And the Lord answered me, and said, Write the vision, and make it plain upon tables, that he may run that readeth it. For the vision is yet for an appointed time, but at the end it*

shall speak, and not lie: though it tarry, wait for it; because
it will surely come, it will not tarry".

A lot of people have given up on dreams that would have changed the world because they did not give it time to mature. One of my favourite poems is Elegy Written in a Country Churchyard in which he laments that the best talent in the world is found in the graveyard:

> *"Perhaps in this neglected spot is laid*
> *Some heart once pregnant with celestial fire;*
> *Hands, that the rod of empire might have sway'd,*
> *Or wak'd to ecstasy the living lyre.*
>
> *But Knowledge to their eyes her ample page*
> *Rich with the spoils of time did ne'er unroll;*
> *Chill Penury repress'd their noble rage,*
> *And froze the genial current of the soul.*

Do not be among those that take their divine purpose to the grave. Patiently work through your vision until it manifests so that you will bring glory to your Maker.

Serve Happily While You Wait

As you wait for your divine purpose to come to blossom, you may find that you are already serving in one or more capacities not specifically related to the purpose. Serve happily while you wait. As time unfolds, you will actually find that God has put you in your current position to prepare you for the great commission that is coming.

David is a shining example. His divine purpose was not to tend sheep. Yet God was teaching him and preparing him in the fields for a higher calling. When the time came, it was not the more illustrious sons that were chosen. The Lord instead *"took David from tending the ewes and lambs and made him the shepherd of Jacob's descendants--God's own people, Israel". (Psalm 78:71).*

Think about it! A young boy covered in earth and grime elevated to high office!

We know of movie starts today that are delighting the public with their acting skills and bringing joy to many. Some of them had very modest beginnings.

Oprah Winfrey, who was raised by her grandmother, was born into poverty in rural Mississippi to a teenage single mother. Winfrey has spoken about experiencing significant hardship as a child, and the fact that she was raped at the age of 9 and became pregnant at 14 (her son died in infancy).

When Winfrey was sent to live with her father in Tennessee, Winfrey found employment in the radio field while still in high school, and would begin her journalism career working as a co-anchor for the local evening news at 19.

Besides positively affecting the lives of billions of viewers around the globe and serving and a role model to many, Oprah is now worth $2.9 billion.

Do not let your current circumstances rob you of your divine purpose.

Give Thanks Always

One of the things I have really found out to be a very powerful empowerment took is gratitude. 1 Thessalonians 5:18 says, *"In everything give thanks: for this is the will of God in Christ Jesus concerning you.*

Wallace D. Wattles, author of *The Science of Getting Rich*, says:

"Many people who order their lives rightly all other ways are kept in poverty by their lack of gratitude. Having received one gift from God, they cut the wires that connect them with Him by failing to make acknowledgement".

Lack of gratitude does not just cut you off riches. It robs you of health, happiness and can eventually rob you of your divine purpose.

Gratitude, or thanksgiving, is predicated on the fact that God is the Source of your life and of everything you need. Second, you believe James 1:17 that "Every good gift and every perfect gift is from above, and comes down from the Father of lights, with whom is no fickleness, neither shadow of turning". Third, you relate yourself to God by expressing genuine and sincere gratitude for what you have received by faith. Gratitude brings you closer to God like nothing else. This guarantees a reaction from the Divine source and good things begin to come your way.

Even in our physical world, gratitude gets you more.

Say a mother makes a promise to her daughter to offer her a pair of shoes. Then one day, even before the mum has actually bought the shoes, the little girl comes in with a had made "thank you" card that reads "mum thank you for the shoes you promised me". Mum will not sleep another day without getting those shoes!

This is the same way that our grateful hearts link us to our Father in heaven, the Eternal source. Wallace D. Wattles in his timeless classic the Science of Getting Rich says, *"the soul that is always grateful lives in closer touch with God than the one who never looks to Him in thankful acknowledgement".*

Each time you awaken and sustain the mental attitude of gratitude, you are drawn into closer touch with the source of all blessings. The nearer you are to the source of your divine purpose, the clearer you purpose will become.

You must have read in your science classes that for every action there is an equal and opposite reaction. This is also a divine principle. Gratitude releases spiritual force which cannot fail to reach the Almighty. Once it reaches Him, there is an instantaneous movement toward you and there are no heights you cannot reach. This is the Divine enablement to do the impossible that is most often referred to as "anointing".

A contemporary example of someone whose gratitude has lifted him to heights untold is global gospel music icon Don Moen. Don himself says "if you thank God for anything you will see it". This must be true because there is not a single album, he produces that does not incorporate the theme of thanksgiving. The result of his outpouring of gratitude is that God has lifted him to literally lead the universe in worship. He has risen through the position of Artistic Director of Integrity Music (now Integrity Media), to Vice President, set up the Don Moen Company, sold upwards of 6 million units in 130 countries and led charitable projects in some of the world's remotest places including Africa.

Only thanksgiving can propel a struggling salesman to such heights. Gratitude can trigger a constant flow of provision in your life and empower you to fulfil your divine purpose.

Make gratitude part of your it divine purpose plan. You will be happy that you did.

CHAPTER 12

IT'S YOUR TURN TO ROCK THE WORLD!

""If one advances confidently in the direction of his
dreams, and endeavours to live the life which he has
imagined, he will meet with a success unexpected
in common hours." Henry David Thoreau

IN CHAPTER 11, we saw that your purpose may take time and
shared with you the need to continue serving where you are with
gratitude. In this brief chapter, I will encourage you to press on
with your divine purpose.

Learn from the Forebears of Divine Purpose

We saw earlier on how some of the forbears of divine purpose
both in the bible and in our time fulfilled their vision against great
and sometimes life-threatening odds. We saw how the Master
Jesus died on the cross to fulfil His mission; we saw how Joseph
accepted apparent humiliation and allowed his wife to carry a baby
he was not the biological father of; we saw how Moses, though
advanced in years, answered the call to serve and liberate God's
people.

Now is your turn. What would you do as you consider your divine
purpose?

Stay the Course and Do Not Faint!

Fulfilling divine purpose or any purpose for that matter, is not a joke. A lot of blind spots hit us in life.

The bible tells the story of Job and how he lost everything including his children.

In 2004, a brother living in Liverpool in the United Kingdom, caught a vision to set up a multi-racial training facility that would bring together all segments of society under one roof to work together. He bought computers with government funding worth £40,000. Everything was going well until one fateful night, a fridge exploded in the IT suite and the project was burned down to ashes in 45 minutes.

The story has been told of Thomas Edison, the father of the electric bulb, and how his lab caught fire and everything was destroyed. His insurance did not cover it. What would you do in the above scenarios? Curse God and die as Job was advised? Declare that "maybe God does not want me to do this" and surrender?

Job, through faith, recovered everything he had lost and then some extras.

The brother who lost the IT suite told the story at a job interview how he managed the crisis and he was offered an executive position in a charity.

Edison sent for his wife and said, "go call your mum to come and see this beautiful scene. All our mistakes are being burnt in the fire and we have the opportunity to start all over again". He discovered the Dictaphone right after that fire and went on to become the world's leading inventor.

Your divine purpose will be tested and you with it. God cannot entrust to a weakling a task that a lot of His creation depends on.

He even tested His only begotten Son Jesus on the cross before conferring the accolade of Messiah on Him.

God's word encourages us not to give up in times of adversity. Joshua 1: 9 says:

> *"Have I not commanded you? Be strong and courageous. Do not be afraid; do not be discouraged, for the LORD your God will be with you wherever you go". "If you fail in times of adversity; then your strength is small." (Proverbs 24:10)*

Our Saviour Jesus fulfilled His divine purpose on earth but it was not easy. At one point the pain became too much until he begged that His Father would take the cup of adversity from Him. Yet He saw it through because He knew the world depended on his mission:

> *"Therefore, since we are surrounded by such a great cloud of witnesses, let us throw off everything that hinders and the sin that so easily entangles. And let us run with perseverance the race marked out for us, fixing our eyes on Jesus, the pioneer and perfecter of faith. For the joy set before him he endured the cross, scorning its shame, and sat down at the right hand of the throne of God. Consider him who endured such opposition from sinners, so that you will not grow weary and lose heart".*

That is why when trials and tribulations line the path of your divine purpose and it seems you cannot carry on, you must:

> *Trust in the LORD with all your heart; and lean not unto your own understanding. In all thy ways acknowledge him, and he shall direct thy paths." (1 Corinthians 16:13).*

Right now, you are capable of walking in that divine purpose that God gave you! Right now, you are able to see through the divine task that is set ahead of you! Right this minute you are ready to join the Hall of Fame of the forerunners of divine purpose! Right now, the world is waiting for you to manifest as the son of God in your divine assignment. Keep going! Never stop! Never give up. March on to victory. 1 Corinthians 16:13says, *"Be on your guard; stand firm in the faith; be courageous; be strong"*.

The world will be a better place because you came!

EPILOGUE

I HAVE THOROUGH enjoyed reading *How To Fulfil Divine Purpose*, by Pastor MKO Oyeneye and I know you have too. I am particularly pleased that the author echoes some points which I highlighted in my book *Why Am I Here: How To Discover Your Purpose And Calling In Life*. In my book, I stated, amongst other things, that "A cemetery is a literal goldmine of the richest ideas...all buried with the one created to accomplish them". This is a terrible tragedy.

My task as a minister of the gospel of our Lord and Saviour Jesus Christ is to work relentlessly to ensure that Christians are not swept away by the winds of mediocrity and end up in dead-end jobs. And other mundane pursuits. I am pleased to read another book on the subject.

I believe the main challenge that lies ahead of you as you read Pastor MKO's book is execution. As Christians, we need to get weary of talking and start doing. *How To Fulfil Your Divine Purpose* is not a novel; it is a wakeup call meant to shake you out of thoughtless acquiescence and propel you in the direction of your divine purpose.

James 1: 23-24 says: *"For if any be a hearer of the word, and not a doer, he is like unto a man beholding his natural face in a glass:*

For he beholdeth himself, and goeth his way, and straightway forgetteth what manner of man he was".

Perhaps you have had a foreboding about what you should be doing and you have never taken the first step. Perhaps you have never even given it thought.

Now is the time. Now is the time to pick up the gauntlet that Pastor MKO is throwing before you. Now is the time to really ask yourself if what you are doing now is worthy of your life on earth.

After reading this book, you may need to make a radical step. People who have made impact in the world have made radical decisions, causing their peers to think they had lost their mind. Why would the General Overseer of JCCI Dr Adekunle Adesina abandon a successful career as a Pharmacist to carry the Holy Book? Why would Ron Kenoly jettison a successful rock star career to create worship music? Why would Jeff Bezos resign from a $95,000-a-year job to set up Amazon?

All these great men heard the call to greatness and decided to make a radical move. In doing so, they made huge sacrifices along the way, but ended up impacting the world.

Now is your turn to arise from slumber and take your God-given position. God has prepared the way for you and He promised that:

> *"[He] will go before thee, and make the crooked places straight: [He] will break in pieces the gates of brass, and cut in sunder the bars of iron". (Isaiah 45:2).*

The world is waiting for the manifestation of your divine purpose! Do not be slothful in your divine purpose! Do not fear and never give up!

The hosts of heaven will rejoice greatly if you find and fulfil that purpose.

Dr Sunday Adelaja
Founder & Senior Pastor
Embassy of God, Kiev
Bestselling Author of *ChurchShift* and *Who Am I and Why Am I Here?*

ABOUT THE AUTHOR

FOR ALMOST THREE decades now, Pastor Matthew Kashman Oluwatosin Oyeneye, has been a significant Team Player/Leader in Jubilee Christian Church International (JCCI) from her headquarters in Nigeria to the United Kingdom where he currently resides. He is a Senior Pastor in JCCI Faith Arena, North London, United Kingdom – The arena for making life relevant, purposeful and eternally rewarding.

For more than two decades, Pastor MKO Oyeneye has been pastoring and teaching faith based and purpose fulfilling gospel of the Kingdom of the Lord Jesus Christ which have transformed many lives.

Called with a specific mandate "to enlighten all men and make plain to them what is the plan (regarding the Gentiles and providing for the salvation of all men) of the mystery kept hidden through the ages and concealed until now in the mind of God Who created all things by Christ Jesus (Eph.3:9)."

Pastor MKO Oyeneye, also known and addressed by his close acquaintances as KASHMAN holds a Higher National Diploma in Accountancy as well as a Master Degree in Business Administration specialising in Financial Management.

He is a Chartered Member of Association of National Accountant of Nigeria (ANAN) and Nigeria Institute of Management (NIM). His Professional/Senior Managerial career span over twenty (20) years at the Ogun State Property & Investment Corporation (OPIC) where he held senior managerial/finance positions before taking up his pastoral responsibilities in United Kingdom. He is currently the Regional Conference Coordinator for UK/

EUROPE. He is also the Assistant General Overseer (Finance) – Jubilee Christian Church International (JCCI).

He is happily married for over 34 years now to a thoroughbred professional Nurse – Pastor (Mrs.) Bernice Aderayo Omotoke (BAO) Oyeneye (Nee Soetan) – A Certified Member of the Royal College of Nursing in England & Wales. Their marriage is blessed with children.

BIBLIOGRAPHY

Books

Adelaja, Sunday, Who Am I? Why Am I Here? Milton Keynes: Golden Pen Limited, 2016

Ash, Mary Kay, Miracles Happen: The Life And Timeless Principles Of The Founder Of Mary Kay Inc. USA: HarperCollins Publishers,1981.

Chopra, Deepak, Unconditional Life: Discovering the Power to Fulfill Your Dreams. London: Bantam Book Publishing, 1989

Danforth, William H, I Dare You! USA: BN Publishing, 2007.

Driver-Bishop, Robert, People of Purpose: 40 Life Lessons From The New Testament. USA: Augsburg Fortress,2005.

Dumont, Theron Q. Dumont, The Power of Concentration. USA: Wilder Publications, 2007.

Gratzon, Fred, The Lazy Way To Success: How To Do Nothing And Accomplish Everything. Iowa: Soma Press, 2003.

Haanel, Charles, The Master Key System. New York: Atria Books, 2008.

Hagin, Kenneth E, Following God's Plan For Your Life, USA: Faith Library Publications, 1996.

Hagin, Kenneth E, Plans Purposes And Pursuits. USA: Faith Library Publications, 1997.

Hurd, Gordon, Christian Prosperity Secrets. UK: Dignity Publishing, 2015.

Jakes, TD, Maximize The Moment: God's Action Plan For Your Life, New York: The Berkley Publishing Group, 1999.

Jakes, TD, Reposition Yourself: Living Life Without Limits. New York: Atria Books, 2007.

Jakes TD, Can You Stand To Be Blessed: Insights To Help You Survive The Peaks And Valleys. USA: Destiny Image, 1994.

Jarrett, RH, It Works: A Concise, Definite, Resultful Plan With Rules, Explanations and Suggestions For Bettering Your Condition In Life. USA: DeVorss & Company, 2000.

Jeffers, Susan, Feel the Fear And Do It Anyway. Reading: CPI Cox & Wyman, 2007.

Johnson, Dani, Spirit Driven Success: Learn Time Tested Biblical Secrets To Create Wealth While Serving Others! USA: Destiny Image, 2009.

Keller, Jeff, Attitude Is Everything: Change Your Attitude...And Change Your Life! USA: International Network Training Institute, 1999.

Kiyosaki, Robert T, Rich Dad, Poor Dad. Arizona: TechPress, 1998.

Levesque, Paul et al, Dream Crafting: The Art of Dreaming Big, The Science of Making It Happen. San Francisco: Berrett-Koehler Publishers, 2003.

Maltz, Maxwell, The New Psycho-Cybernetics: The Original Science of Self-Improvement And Success That Has Changed The Lives of 30 Million People. London: Prentice Hall Press, 2002.

Meyer, Joyce, How To Succeed At Being Yourself: Finding The Confidence To Fulfill Your Destiny. USA: Warner Faith Publishers, 1999.

Munroe, Miles, In Pursuit of Purpose. USA: Destiny Image Publishers, 2015.

Murphy, Joseph, The Power of Your Subconscious Mind. USA: Wilder Publications, 2007.

Musengi, Florence, Woman At The Top: Challenging Women Everywhere To Be The Best They Can. UK: Dignity Publishing, 2015.

Neville (With Joe Vitale), At Your Command. USA: Morgan James, 2005.

Neville, Awakened Imagination: The Power That Makes Achievement and Attainment Inevitable. USA: De Vorss Publications, 1954.

Neville, Feeling Is The Secret. USA: BN Publishing, 2007.

Neville, Resurrection: Imagine Your Dream As Reality...Begin There and Live. USA: De Vorss Publications, 1966.

Nightingale, Earl, Lead The Field: Lesson 1, The Magic & Acres of Diamonds. USA: BN Publishing, 2006.

Osteen, Joel, Your Best Life Now: 7 Steps To Living At Your Full Potential. USA: Warner Faith, 2004.

Rees Erik, S.H.A.P.E: Finding And Fulfilling Your Unique Purpose For Life. USA: Sondervan Publishing, 2006.

Rogak, Lisa, Barack Obama In His Own Words. London: JR Books, 2009.

Ron, Jim, The Five Major Pieces to the Life Puzzle. Texas: Dickinson Press, 1991.

Shwartz, David J, The Magic of Thinking Big. New York: Prentice Hall, 1965.

Sweetland, Ben, I Will: A Practical Guide for Utilizing The Powerful Forces of Your Subconscious Mind. California: Wilshire Book Company, 1960.

Warren, Rick, The Purpose Driven Church: Growth Without Compromising Your Message and Mission. UAS: Zondervan Publishing,1995.

Warren, Rick, The Purpose Driven Life: What On Earth Am I Here For? USA: Zondervan, 2002.

Scripture Reference Resources

King James Bible. Thomas Nelson Publishers, 1977.

Swaggart, Jimmy, The Expositor's Study Bible. Jimmy Swaggart Ministries, 2005.

The Thompson Chain-Reference Bible (King James Version). Kirkbridge Bible Company, Inc. 1988.

CPSIA information can be obtained
at www.ICGtesting.com
Printed in the USA
BVHW081149100719
553057BV00005B/423/P